Comp...
Food & ...
in Fra...

General Editor
Simon Collin

French Editor
Françoise Laurendeau

First published in Great Britain 2002 by
Aspect Guides, an imprint of Peter Collin Publishing Ltd
32-34 Great Peter Street, London, SW1P 2DB

British Library Cataloguing-in-Publication Data

A catalogue record for this book is available from the British Library

ISBN 1-904012-05-1

Typeset by PCP
Printed and bound in Italy by Legoprint
Cover artwork by Sue Bailey

Companion to
Food & Drink
in France

General Editor
Simon Collin

French Editor
Françoise Laurendeau

Contents

Introduction   6
    Types of restaurant   6
    Closing times   6
    Tipping   7
    Public holidays in France   7
    Booking   7
    Meal times   7
    Rating schemes   7

Useful French phrases   9
    Menu   9
    Getting to a restaurant   9
    Ordering   10
    Drinks   11
    Complaints   12
    Paying   12
    Numbers   12

French-English menu dictionary   13

English-French menu dictionary   55

Wines and spirits   101
    Wine regions   102
    Wine glossary   107

Classic French sauces   113

Retaurant notes   123
    New restaurants   124
    New terms   126

Preface

If you have ever ordered from a menu written in French without being completely sure what you were asking for, then you need this pocket dictionary!

We have compiled this book to provide an essential pocket companion for any traveller who likes to know what they are ordering and eating. And unlike many other dictionaries, the text is fully bilingual - to and from English, so that you can easily translate a menu or ask for a favourite dish or a particular ingredient.We have included over 1,500 dishes and ingredients, with a special chapters on wine and French sauces (an essential part of any classic French dish).

This pocket book is structured in four main sections:
> English-French menu dictionary
> French-English menu dictionary
> French wines and wine terms
> Classic French sauces

The dictionary includes several pages of useful phrases. These have been selected to help you to find a restaurant, ask for the table that you want, order your meal, pay the bill - and, if necessary, complain.

Finally, as you travel you will doubtless find new local dishes and local names for ingredients - in our experience, this is particularly so with local names for different types of fish. At the back of the book we have included pages where you can record new terms and their meanings. If you find interesting new terms that are not in this book, we would love to hear from you; please let us know and we will try and include the terms in future editions. Send any new terms (or comments on local variations of expressions) to: **food@aspectguides.com**

Introduction

Types of restaurant

une auberge	*hotel-restaurant, usually in the country*
un bar	*serves alcoholic drinks*
un bistrot	*café-restaurant, serves drinks and simple meals*
une brasserie	*café-restaurant, choice of beer and simple meals*
un café	*serves alcoholic drinks and coffee, some serve ice cream*
un café-restaurant	*serves alcoholic drinks, serves meals*
une cafétéria	*self-service restaurant providing simple meals*
un restaurant	*proper dining room; quality can vary*
un restaurant d'autoroute	*motorway restaurant, often a cafeteria*
un restaurant gastronomique	*high quality food, though sometimes no choice of menu, often more expensive*
un salon de thé	*shop selling cakes with a few tables to have tea or coffee*

Closing Times

As shops tend to shut abruptly for lunch, so, oddly, do some restaurants. Many smaller restaurants have a weekly closure timetable (fermeture hebdomadaire) - closing, commonly, on Sunday and Monday.

Tipping

Tipping is relatively straightforward: bills are often stamped 's.t.c.' (service, taxes, compris) and it means what it says - all service and taxes included. The only exception perhaps is to leave the small change in the saucer at a bar (if you are eating at the bar rather than at a table).

Public holidays in France

New Year's Day
Easter Sunday and Monday
Labour Day, 1 May
VE Day, 8 May
Ascension Day
Whit Sunday and Monday
France's National Day, 14 July
The Assumption, 15 August
All Saints' Day, 1 November
Armistice Day, 11 November
Christmas Day

Booking

If any of the national holidays above are part of your holiday, you should book well ahead for a place in a restaurant. Outside Paris, you should also book in advance for Sunday lunch when large families settle down soon after mid-day to enjoy a long, noisy lunch. And don't imagine you can squeeze in for a second sitting, except for some Parisian or tourist-driven restaurants, there is no such thing.

Meals and eating times

07:00 - 09:00	petit déjeuner	*breakfast*
12:00 - 14:00	déjeuner	*lunch*
19:30 - 22:30	dîner	*dinner*

Restaurant rating schemes

Toques (chef's hats) (five toques = de luxe, one toque = fourth-class);
Michelin stars (three-stars = exceptional, one-star = very good)

Useful French Phrases

Menu

Menus are usually split into five sections:

potage *or* hors-d'oeuvre	*soup or starter*
entrée	*first course*
plat principal	*main course*
fromage	*cheese course*
dessert	*dessert*

Shorter menus might have just three sections:

entrée	*first course*
plat principal	*main course*
dessert	*dessert*

Getting to a restaurant

Can you recommend a good restaurant?	*Quel restaurant nous recommandez-vous?*
I would like to reserve a table for this evening	*J'aimerais réserver une table pour ce soir*
Do you have a table for three/four people	*Avez-vous une table pour trois/quatre (personnes)?*
We would like the table for 8 o'clock	*Nous aimerions réserver une table pour 20 heures*
Could we have a table....?	*Auriez-vous une table de libre...?*
by the window	*près de la fenêtre*
outside	*dehors/à l'extérieur*
on the terrace	*sur la terrasse*
in the non-smoking area	*dans la section non-fumeurs*
in the smoking area	*dans la section fumeurs*
What time do you open?	*à quelle heure ouvrez-vous?*
Could you order a taxi for me?	*pourriez-vous me faire venir un taxi?*

Ordering

Waiter/waitress !		*Garçon! / Mademoiselle !*
What do you recommend?		*Que nous proposez-vous?*
What are the specials of the day?		*Quels sont les spéciaux du jour?*
Is this the fixed-price menu?		*C'est le menu à prix fixe?*
Can we see the à-la-carte menu?		*Vous avez aussi un menu à la carte?*
Is this fresh?		*Est-ce frais?*
Is this local?		*Est-ce une spécialité de la région?*
I would like a/an ...		*J'aimerais un/une...*
Could I/we have ... please?		*Pourriez-vous me/nous donner...*
	an ashtray	*un cendrier*
	the bill	*l'addition*
	our coats	*nos manteaux*
	a cup	*une tasse*
	a fork	*une fourchette*
	a glass	*un verre*
	a knife	*un couteau*
	the menu	*le menu*
	a napkin	*une serviette*
	a plate	*une assiette*
	a spoon	*une cuillère*
	a toothpick	*un cure-dents*
	the wine list	*la carte des vins*
May I have some ...?		*J'aimerais avoir/pourriez-vous m'apporter*
	bread	*du pain*
	butter	*du beurre*
	ice	*de la glace*
	(slice of) lemon	*une tranche de citron*
	milk	*du lait*
	pepper	*du poivre*
	salt	*du sel*
	sugar	*du sucre*
	water	*de l'eau*
I would like it ...		*Je le/la préférerais/je l'aimerais*
	baked	*cuit(e) au four*
	fried	*frit(e)*
	grilled	*grillé(e)*

poached	*poché(e)*
smoked	*fumé(e)*
steamed	*(cuit(e)) à la vapeur*
boiled	*cuit(e) à l'eau/à l'anglaise*
roast	*rôti(e)*
very rare	*bleu*
rare	*saignant(e)*
medium	*à point/rose*
well-done	*bien cuit(e)*

Drinks

Can I see the wine list, please?	*Puis-je avoir la carte des vins s'il vous plaît?*
I would like a/an...	*J'aimerais avoir*
aperitif	*un apéritif*
another	*un deuxième; encore un(e)*
I would like a glass of ...	*Puis-je avoir un verre de/d'*
red wine	*vin rouge*
white wine	*vin blanc*
rose wine	*vin rosé*
sparkling wine	*vin mousseux*
still water	*eau plate*
sparkling water	*eau gazeuse*
tap water	*eau du robinet*
With lemon	*avec du citron*
With ice	*avec de la glace*
With water	*avec de l'eau*
Neat	*sans eau ni glace*
I would like a bottle of....	*Donnez-moi une bouteille de*
this wine	*ce vin-ci*
house red	*de vin rouge maison*
house white	*de vin blanc maison*
Is this wine ...?	*Est-ce un vin ...?*
very dry	*très sec*
dry	*sec*
sweet	*doux/sucré*
local	*de la région*
This wine is	*Le vin...*
not very good	*n'est pas très bon*
not very cold	*n'est pas très frais*

Complaints

This is not what I ordered		*Ce n'est pas ce que j'ai commandé*
I asked for ...		*J'ai commandé...*
Could I change this?		*Est-ce que je peux le changer pour autre chose?*
The meat is ...		*la viande...*
	overdone	*est trop cuite*
	underdone	*n'est pas assez cuite*
	tough	*est dure*
I don't like this		*je n'aime pas ça*
The food is cold		*tout est froid*
This is not fresh		*ce n'est pas frais*
What is taking so long?		*pourquoi est-ce si long?*
This is not clean		*ce n'est pas propre*

Paying

Could I have the bill?	*Pourrez-vous m'apportez l'addition*
I would like to pay	*Garçon, l'addition*
Can I charge it to my room?	*vous l'ajoutez à ma note d'hôtel?*
We would like to pay separately	*chacun paye sa part*
There's a mistake in the bill	*je crois qu'il y a une erreur sur la facture*
What's this amount for?	*ce montant représente quoi?*
Is service included?	*le service est-il compris?*
Do you accept traveller's cheques?	*acceptez-vous les chèques de voyage?*
Can I pay by credit card?	*vous acceptez les cartes de crédit?*

Numbers

0	*zéro*		6	*six*
1	*un*		7	*sept*
2	*deux*		8	*huit*
3	*trois*		9	*neuf*
4	*quatre*		10	*dix*
5	*cinq*			

French-English

La Maison Blanche

Aa

abats giblets
abattis *[de volaille]* giblets
abricot apricot
absinthe absinthe
accompagnement *[garniture]* trimmings
acide sharp
addition bill, *[US]* check
agneau lamb
aiglefin, églefin haddock
   aiglefin fumé *[haddock]* smoked haddock
aigre sour
aigre-doux (-douce) sweet and sour
aiguillat, chien de mer dog fish
ail garlic
aillé(e) garlicky
ailloli, aïoli aïloli sauce
airelle myrtille blueberry
airelle rouge small cranberry
algue seaweed
allumettes matches
   allumettes au fromage (fine) cheese straws
   pommes allumettes matchstick potatoes
alose shad
alouette lark *[bird]*
   alouette sans tête beef olive
aloyau *[faux-filet]* sirloin
amande (douce) almond
   aux amandes with almonds
   pâte d'amandes almond paste
amer (amère) bitter
amuse-gueule *[hors-d'oeuvre]* hors-d'oeuvre; *[US]* appetizer
ananas pineapple

anchois anchovy
   anchois de Norvège sprat
andouillette pig tripe *[stuffed with chitterlings, pork meat, onions, seasoning, etc.]*
aneth dill
ange de mer angel fish
anglaise, à l' plain boiled *[vegetables]*
angélique angelica
anguille eel
   anguille fumée smoked eel
anis aniseed
anone *[pomme canelle]* custard apple
apéritif aperitif; *[US]* appetizer
arachide peanut
arêtes (de poisson) (fish) bones
arôme (d'un vin) aroma
arrow-root arrowroot
artichaut artichoke
   fond d'artichaut artichoke bottom
asperge asparagus
   pointes d'asperges asparagus tips
aspic aspic *[galantine]*
assaisonnement seasoning
assiette plate
   assiette anglaise, assiette de
   viandes froides assorted cold meat; *[US]* cold cuts
   assiette de viandes grillées mixed grill
aubergine aubergine; *[US]* eggplant
autruche ostrich
aveline filbert
avocat avocado
avoine oats

Bb

baba au rhum rum baba
bacon *[lard fumé]* bacon
baguette *[pain]* French bread
baguettes *[chinoises]* chopsticks
balaou saury
baleine whale
ballottine faggot
banana split banana split
banane banana
   bananes flambées banana flambé
   banane verte *[plantain]* plantain
bar *[loup de mer]* sea bass
barbecue barbecue
barbue brill
barquette small tart *[shaped like a boat]*
basilic basil
baudroie *[lotte de mer]* monkfish
bavarois bavarian cream
bavette, bavoir (child's) bib
bécasse woodcock
bécassine snipe
béchamel, sauce béchamel white sauce, béchamel sauce
beignet *[pâte frite et sucrée]* doughnut
   beignet fourré à la confiture jam doughnut
   beignet *[fruit enrobé de pâte frite]* fritter
   beignet de bananes banana fritter
   beignet de pommes apple fritter
bergamote bergamot
bette, blette chard
betterave beetroot
beurre butter
   avec (du) beurre; au beurre with butter

sans beurre   without butter
beurre clarifié *[cuisine indienne]*   ghee
beurre d'anchois   anchovy butter
beurre de cacah(o)uètes, d'arachides   peanut butter
beurre de cacao   cocoa butter
beurre de truffes   truffle butter
beurre fondu   melted butter
beurre noisette   brown butter
beurre sans sel   unsalted butter

bien cuit(e)   well done

bière   beer
  bière (à la) pression   draught beer
  bière anglaise blonde   ale
  bière anglaise pression   bitter (beer)
  bière blonde   lager

bifteck, steak   steak; *[US]* beefsteak

bigorneau   winkle

biscotte   crispbread

biscotte *[pour bébé]*   rusk

biscuits *[gâteaux secs]*   biscuit; *[US]* cookies
  biscuits à la cuillère   sponge biscuits

bisque de homard   lobster bisque

blanc d'oeuf   egg white

blanchaille   whitebait

blanchir   to blanch

blanc-manger   blancmange

blé   wheat
  blé concassé   bulgur wheat, bulgar wheat
  blé noir *[sarrasin]*   buckwheat

blennie   butterfish

blinis   blinis

boeuf   beef
  boeuf de conserve   corned beef
  boeuf en daube   beef casserole
  rôti de boeuf *[rosbif]*   roast beef

bogue *[poisson]*   bogue *[fish]*

boisson (gazeuse) non alcoolisée   soft drink

boîte (de conserve)   tin; *[US]* can
  en boîte   tinned; *[US]* canned

bol bowl
bombe bombe
bonbon sweet; *[US]* candy
bonite bonito; skipjack
bordeaux rouge claret
bordelaise, à la with wine, bone marrow, mushrooms, artichokes
bouchée (feuilletée) vol au vent
   bouchée à la reine chicken vol au vent
boudin blanc sausage of finely ground white meat
boudin noir black pudding
bouillabaisse (Mediterranean) fish stew
bouillir to boil
bouilli(e) *[cuit(e) à l'eau, à l'anglaise]* boiled
bouillon broth
   bouillon de boeuf beef tea, beef broth
   bouillon de légumes vegetable broth, castor broth
boule de glace ice cream scoop
boulette de pâte dumpling
boulette de viande meat ball
bouquet (d'un vin) aroma
bouquet garni bouquet garni *[mixed herbs]*
bouquet *[crevette rose]* prawn
bourguignonne, à la with red wine, mushrooms, small onions, bacon
bourrache borage
bouteille bottle
   bouteille d'eau (minérale) bottle of (mineral) water
   bouteille de vin bottle of wine
   demi-bouteille half-bottle
braisé(e) braised
braiser to braise
brème bream
brème de mer sea bream
brioche brioche
brochet pike
brochette skewer
brocoli broccoli
brugnon *[nectarine]* nectarine
brûlé(e) burnt

brûler   to burn
buccin   whelk
bûche de Noël   Christmas log
buffet   buffet

Cc

cabillaud   (fresh) cod
cacah(o)uète   peanut
cacao   cocoa, chocolate
café   coffee
   café au lait   coffee with milk
   café complet   continental breakfast
   café crème, un crème   (large) coffee with cream or milk
   café décaféiné; un déca   decaffeinated coffee; decaf
   café express   espresso, expresso coffee
   café filtre   filter coffee
   café noir   black coffee
   café soluble, instantané   instant coffee
caféine   caffeine
   sans caféine *[décaféiné]*   caffeine-free, decaffeinated
cafetière   coffee pot
caille   quail
   oeufs de caille   quails eggs
cake   fruit cake
calmar *[encornet]*   squid
camomille *[infusion de, tisane de]*   camomile (tea)
canapés   canapés
canard   duck *[domestic]*
   canard à l'orange   duck with oranges
   canard sauvage   wild duck
caneton   duckling
canneberge   cranberry

cannelle cinnamon

cantaloup cantaloup (melon)

cappucino cappucino coffee

câpres capers

carafe carafe
   carafe d'eau carafe of water, jug of water

caramel caramel
   caramel (au beurre) toffee

cardamome cardamom

carotte carrot

carpe carp

carré rack
   carré [d'agneau, de porc, etc.] rack of ribs
   carré d'agneau rack of lamb

carrelet plaice

carte des vins wine list

carthame safflower

cartilage [croquant] gristle

casher, kasher kosher

cassate cassata

casserole casserole

cassis blackcurrant

catalane, à la with tomatoes, black olives, garlic

cavaillon honeydew melon

caviar caviar

cédrat citron

céleri celery

céleri-rave celeriac

cendrier ashtray

cèpe cep; porcini mushroom

céréales (froides) (breakfast) cereal

cerfeuil chervil

cerise cherry
   cerise confite glacé cherry
   cerise noire black cherry

cervelas saveloy

cervelle brains
   cervelle de veau calf's brains

chaise   chair

chambré(e)   at room temperature

champagne   champagne

champignon   mushroom
   champignons de Paris   button mushrooms

chandelier   candlestick

chandelle   candle

chanterelle   chanterelle *[mushroom]*

Chantilly   (with) whipped cream

chapelure   breadcrumbs

chapon   capon

charbon de bois   charcoal

charlotte   charlotte
   charlotte aux pommes   apple charlotte

châtaigne, marron   sweet chestnut
   châtaigne d'eau   water chestnut

Chateaubriand, Chateaubriant   Chateaubriand *[thick piece of grilled fillet of beef]*

chaud(e)   hot *[not cold]*

chaud-froid   jelly, aspic *[savoury]*
   chaud-froid de poulet   chicken in jelly, aspic of chicken

(faire) chauffer   to heat up

chausson (aux pommes, etc.)   turnover
   chausson aux pommes   apple turnover

chef   chef, cook

cherry brandy *[liqueur de cerise]*   cherry brandy

cheveux d'ange   angel hair (pasta)

chèvre   goat

chevreuil   venison *[deer]*
   chevreuil *[à la scandinave]*   reindeer

chicorée frisée   endive, frisée salad

chili con carne *[plat mexicain]*   chilli-con-carne

chinchard   horse mackerel

chips, pommes chips   (potato) crisps; *[US]* chips

chocolat   chocolate, cocoa
   chocolat au lait   milk chocolate
   chocolat blanc   white chocolate
   chocolat noir   dark chocolate

un chocolat *[bonbon]* a chocolate
un chocolat *[une tasse]* a cup of cocoa, of hot chocolate
choix de légumes, légumes variés assorted vegetables
chou cabbage
  chou blanc white cabbage
  chou de Chine chinese cabbage
  chou vert *[pommé]* green cabbage
  chou vert frisé *[non pommé]* kale
  chou vert frisé *[pommé]* savoy cabbage
  chou rouge red cabbage
choucroute pickled cabbage
chou-fleur cauliflower
  chou-fleur sauce Mornay, au
  gratin cauliflower cheese
chou-rave kohlrabi
choux de Bruxelles brussels sprouts
ciboule, cive spring onion; *[US]* scallion
ciboulette; civette chives
cidre (de pomme) cider
  cidre de poire perry
citron lemon
  citron vert *[lime]* lime
citronnelle lemon grass
civet de lièvre jugged hare
clémentine clementine
clou de girofle clove
cochon de lait, porcelet suck(l)ing pig
coeur heart
cognac brandy
coing quince
colin *[merlu]* hake
colin *[lieu noir]* saithe
compote de fruits stewed fruit
compris(e) included
compte account
concombre cucumber
condiment condiment
confit de canard, d'oie duck, goose preserved in own fat

confit(e) *[fruit, etc.]*   candied

confiture   jam

   confiture de fraises   strawberry jam

congre *[anguille de mer]*   conger eel

conserves   preserves

consommé   clear soup, consommé (soup)

   consommé froid   cold consommé

   consommé en tasse, en gelée   jellied consommé

coq au vin   chicken cooked in red wine

coques   cockles

coquetier   egg cup

coquille St Jacques   scallop

coriandre   coriander

cornet (de glace)   (ice cream) cone, cornet

cornichon   gherkin

   cornichon saumuré, au vinaigre   pickled gherkin

côte   chop

   côte de porc   pork chop

côtelette   cutlet, chop

   côtelette d'agneau   lamb chop

côtes   ribs

   côtes de boeuf   ribs of beef

coupe glacée   bowl of ice cream; sundae

courge   squash, marrow *[vegetable]*

courgette   courgette; *[US]* zucchini

court-bouillon   fish broth

couscous   couscous

couteau   knife

couvert   cutlery

crabe *[tourteau]*   crab

   crabe décortiqué   prepared crab

   crabe froid à l'anglaise, à la russe   dressed crab

crème   cream

   crème (légère; épaisse)   single cream; double cream

   crème aigre   sour cream

   crème Chantilly, crème fouettée   whipped cream

   crème fleurette   top of the milk; single cream

   crème fraîche   crème fraîche

   à la crème   with cream; with cream sauce

un crème, un café crème (large) coffee with cream or milk

crème (de) *[velouté]*   cream of
   crème d'asperges cream of asparagus soup
   crème de tomates cream of tomato soup
   crème de volaille cream of chicken soup

crème anglaise custard sauce

crème caramel crème caramel *[baked custard with caramel sauce]*

crème pâtissière confectioner's cream

crémeux (-euse) creamy

créole *[savoury]* with rice, tomatoes, pepper; *[sweet]* with orange peel

crêpe pancake

cresson cress
   cresson de fontaine watercress

crevette (grise) shrimp
   crevette rose king prawn
   crevettes mayonnaise shrimp cocktail

croque-madame fried cheese and ham sandwich topped with a fried egg

croque-monsieur fried cheese and ham sandwich

croquette de poisson fish cake
   croquettes de pommes de terre croquette potatoes

croûtons croutons

cru(e) raw, uncooked

crumble crumble

crustacés shellfish

cube: en cubes diced *[cubed]*

cuillère, cuiller spoon
   cuillère à café coffee spoon
   cuillère à dessert tablespoon
   cuillère à soupe soup spoon
   cuillère à thé tea spoon

cuisses de grenouilles frog's legs

cuit(e) cooked; done
   cuit(e) au four baked
   cuit(e) à grande friture deep-fried
   cuit(e) à la vapeur steamed
   pas assez cuit(e) underdone
   trop cuit(e) overdone

cumin cumin (seed)

   cumin des prés, carvi   caraway (seeds)
curcuma   turmeric
cure-dent(s)   toothpick
curry, cari   curry

Dd

dame blanche   chocolate sunday with Chantilly
darne de saumon   salmon steak
datte   date
dé: en dés   diced, cubed, chopped
décaféiné   decafeinated
   café décaféiné; un déca   decafeinated coffee; decaf
découper   to carve
défense de fumer   no smoking
dégeler   to thaw
déjeuner *[lunch]*   lunch; to have lunch
délicieux (-euse)   delicious
désossé(e) *[en filets]*   filleted
désossé(e) *[sans os, sans arête]*   boned
désosser *[lever les filets; enlever les os, les arêtes]*   to fillet; to debone
dessert   dessert
desservir (la table)   to clear up
diable (à la)   devilled
   rognons à la (sauce) diable   devilled kidneys
   sauce (à la) diable   devilled sauce
dinde   turkey
   dinde rôtie   roast turkey
dîner *[midi]*   lunch
dîner *[soir]*   dinner, supper
dorade (aux sourcils d'or)   gilthead bream
dorée *[poisson]*   john dory

French-English

dorer, faire dorer   to brown
dormeur *[tourteau]*   crab
Dubarry, à la   with cauliflower

Ee

eau   water
   eau de seltz   soda water
   eau de source; eau minérale   spring water; mineral water
   eau en bouteille   bottled water
   eau gazeuse   sparkling water, fizzy water
   eau glacée, très froide   iced water
   eau minérale   mineral water
   eau plate   still (mineral) water
   sans eau ni glace   neat; *[US]* straight *[whisky, etc.]*
eau de vie de prunelle   sloe gin
ébréché(e) *[verre, assiette]*   chipped (glass, plate)
échalote   shallot
éclair   éclair
   éclair au chocolat   chocolate eclair
écorce (de citron, etc.)   (lemon, etc.) peel
   écorce confite   candied peel
   écorce râpée *[zeste]*   grated peel, zest
écrevisse   crayfish
édulcorant   sweetener
endive   chicory
entrecôte   beef steak
entrée   starter
entremets salé   savoury
épaule *[palette]*   shoulder
éperlan   smelt
épice   spice
épicé(e)   spicy

épinard   spinach
   épinards en purée   creamed spinach
escalope   escalope
   escalope de dinde   turkey escalope
   escalope de veau   veal escalope
escargot   snail
espadon   swordfish
esquimau   ice lolly
estragon   taragon, tarragon
esturgeon   sturgeon

Ff

faînes   beech nuts
faisan   pheasant
farce   stuffing
farci(e)   stuffed (with)
farine   flour
   farine d'avoine   oatmeal
   farine de maïs   cornmeal, polenta
faux filet   sirloin steak
fécule de maïs   cornflour
fenouil   fennel
fermier *[oeuf, poulet]*   free range, farm *[egg, chicken]*
fermière   with carrots, turnip, onion, celery
feuille de laurier   bay leaf
feuilles de vigne   vine leaves
fève   bean
   fève des marais, grosse fève   broad bean
ficelle   French bread *[very thin]*
ficelle picarde   ham rolled in pancake served with white sauce
figue   fig

filet fillet; tenderloin
  filet de porc pork tenderloin
  filet de boeuf fillet of beef; *[US]* beef tenderloin
  filet de boeuf en croûte beef Wellington
  filet de volaille breast of chicken or turkey
fines herbes herbs
flageolet flageolet (beans)
flambé(e) flambé
flan baked custard
flet flounder
flétan halibut
  flétan noir black halibut, Greenland halibut
flocons flakes
  flocons d'avoine rolled oats
florentine with spinach
foie liver
  foies de poulets, de volaille chicken livers
  foie de veau calf's liver
  foie d'oie, foie gras goose liver pâté
fondant fondant
  fondant au chocolat chocolate fudge (icing)
fondue fondue
forestière with mushrooms, bacon, sauté potatoes
forêt-noire black forest gateau
four oven
  cuit(e) au four baked
  pommes au four baked apples
fourchette fork
fourré(e) (à, au, aux) filled (with), stuffed (with)
frais (fraîche) fresh
fraise strawberry
  fraise des bois, fraise sauvage wild strawberry
  glace à la fraise strawberry ice cream
framboise raspberry
friand puffed pastry filled with meat
  friand à la saucisse sausage roll
  friand au jambon ham roll *[in puffed pastry]*
fricassée stew
  fricassée de boeuf stewed steak; beef stew

frire to fry

frit(e) fried

frites (potato) chips; *[US]* french fries

friture de poissons mixed fried fish

froid(e) cold

fromage cheese
  fromage 'cottage' cottage cheese
  fromage à la crème cream cheese
  fromage à pâte dure hard cheese
  fromage à pâte molle soft cheese
  fromage bleu blue cheese
  fromage de (lait de) brebis ewe's milk cheese
  fromage de chèvre goat's cheese
  fromage de lait entier full-fat cheese
  plateau à fromage; plateau de fromages cheese board

fromage de tête brawn

fruit fruit
  fruits confits crystallised fruit
  fruits frais fresh fruit
  fruits de mer seafood; shellfish

fumé(e) smoked; cured

Gg

galantine galantine

galette de sarrasin buckwheat pancake

garçon, serveur waiter

gaspacho gazpacho

gâteau cake, gateau
  gâteau à la crème cream cake
  gâteau au fromage blanc cheesecake
  gâteau au gingembre ginger cake
  gâteau aux carottes carrot cake

French-English

gâteau de Noël *[anglais]* Christmas cake
gâteau mousseline sponge cake
gâteau quatre-quarts pound cake
gâteau renversé upside-down cake
gâteau roulé swiss roll
gâteaux secs biscuits; *[US]* cookies
gaufres waffles
gaufrette wafer
gélatine gelatine
gelée jelly
gelée à la menthe mint jelly
gelée de groseilles redcurrant jelly
genièvre *[eau-de-vie]* gin
baie de genièvre juniper berry
génoise sponge cake
génoise au citron; gâteau de Savoie madeira cake
germes de luzerne alfalfa sprouts
germes de soja bean sprouts
gibier (à plume; à poil) game
gigot d'agneau leg of lamb
gingembre ginger
gîte à la noix silverside
glace ice
avec glace with ice; *[whisky, etc.]* with ice, on the rocks
sans eau ni glace neat; *[US]* straight *[whisky, etc.]*
glace *[crème glacée]* ice cream
glace à la vanille vanilla ice cream
glace, glaçage *[pour gâteaux]* icing
glacé(e) *[very cold]* icy cold
glacé(e) *[de sucre, etc.]* glazed
glaçon ice cube
glouteron, bardane burdock
glucides *[hydrates de carbone]* carbohydrate
gnocchi Parmentier potato dumpling
gombo gumbo, okra, ladies finger
goujon *[poisson]* gudgeon
goujons de poulet goujons, slivers of chicken
goulash, goulasch goulash

gousse de vanille vanilla pod/bean

goyave guava

graines de sésame sesame seeds

granité sherbet; granita

gras fat *[noun]*
   qui contient peu de gras low in fat

gras (grasse) fat *[adj]*

gras-double tripe

gratin dauphinois scalloped potatoes *[US]*

gratiné(e), au gratin browned; *[US]* au gratin

grenade pomegranate

grenadine grenadine

gril grill *[noun]*

grillade grilled piece of meat
   grillade de veau grilled veal chop

grillé(e) grilled
   grillé(e) au barbecue barbecued
   grillé(e) au charbon de bois charcoal-grilled

griller to grill

grive thrush

grondin gurnard

groseille à maquereau gooseberry
   groseille rouge redcurrant

grouse grouse

guimauve marshmallow

Hh

hachis *[viande hachée]* minced meat
   hachis de boeuf minced beef; *[US]* ground beef
   hachis Parmentier shepherd's pie

haddock *[aiglefin fumé]* smoked haddock

hamburger hamburger

hareng herring
   hareng bouffi bloater
   hareng mariné pickled herring
   hareng saur, fumé kipper
   hareng roulé (mariné) rollmop (herring)

harenguet sprat

haricot bean
   haricots blancs haricot beans
   haricots blancs aux tomates baked beans
   haricots grimpants runner beans
   haricots noirs black beans
   haricots rouges kidney beans, red beans
   haricots verts green beans, french beans

heure du thé tea-time

homard lobster

hongroise, à la with paprika, fresh cream

hors d'oeuvre hors d'oeuvre; *[US]* appetizer

hot dog *[saucisse de Francfort dans un petit pain]* hot dog

huile oil
   à l'huile with oil
   huile d'arachide peanut oil, groundnut oil
   huile de tournesol sunflower oil
   huile d'olive olive oil
   huile d'olive vierge virgin olive oil

huître oyster

hydromel mead

hyposodé(e) low-salt (diet)

Ii

ide ide *[fish]*
igname yam
îles flottantes floating islands
infusion herbal tea
ingrédients ingredients

Jj

jambon ham
   jambon blanc (slice of boiled) ham
   jambon de Parme parma ham
   jambon fumé (désossé) gammon
   jambon poché boiled ham
jarret knuckle
jaune d'oeuf egg yolk
julienne julienne
jus (de fruits) juice
   jus de citron lemon juice
   jus de fruits fruit juice
   jus d'orange orange juice
   jus de pomme apple juice
   jus de tomate tomato juice

Kk

kaki   date plum, kaki
kasher *[casher]*   kosher
kébab *[brochette]*   kebab
ketchup *[sauce tomate]*   ketchup
kiwi   kiwi fruit
kumquat   kumquat

Ll

lait   milk
   avec (du) lait; au lait   with milk
   sans lait   without milk
   lait condensé   condensed milk
   lait de beurre *[babeurre]*   buttermilk
   lait de brebis   ewe's milk
   lait de chèvre   goat's milk
   lait de coco   coconut milk
   lait de vache   cow's milk
   lait écrémé   skimmed milk
   lait entier   full-cream milk
laitance   soft roe
laitue *[salade]*   lettuce
   laitue iceberg   iceberg lettuce
   laitue romaine   cos lettuce
langouste   crawfish, spiny lobster
langoustine   Dublin bay prawn
langue   tongue

langue de boeuf ox tongue
lapin; lapereau rabbit; young rabbit
lard de poitrine streaky bacon
    lard fumé smoked bacon
lasagne lasagne
lavande lavender
leberwurst liver sausage
légume vegetable
    légumes verts green vegetables, greens
    légumes variés, choix de légumes assorted vegetables
légumineuses pulses
lentille lentil
letchi, litchi lychee
lieu jaune pollack, lythe
lieu noir saithe
lièvre hare
limande dab
limande-sole lemon sole
lime *[citron vert]* lime
limonade *[citron pressé]* lemonade
lingue ling
liqueur liqueur
litchi, letchi lychee
loganberry loganberry
longe (de veau, porc, chevreuil) loin (of veal, pork, venison)
lotte (d'eau douce) burbot
    lotte de mer *[baudroie]* monkfish
loup bass
    loup de mer sea bass
lyonnaise with sautéed onions

French-English

Mm

macaron macaroon

macaroni macaroni

macédoine de fruits fruit salad; fruit cocktail
   macédoine de légumes mixed vegetable

mâche lamb's lettuce

macis mace

madère *[vin]* madeira

maïs *[plant]* maize; *[US]* corn
   maïs (en épis, en grains) sweetcorn
   épi de maïs, maïs en épi corn on the cob *[sweetcorn]*
   farine de maïs cornmeal
   maïs soufflé popcorn
   semoule de maïs *[polenta]* polenta

malt malt

mandarine mandarin

mange-touts mangetout, sugar snap peas

mangouste, mangoustan mangosteen

mangue mango

maquereau mackerel
   maquereau mariné au vin
   blanc mackerel marinated in white wine

marcassin young boar

marché market

margarine margarine

mariné(e) marinated

marjolaine marjoram

marmelade, confiture d'oranges (orange) marmalade

marron sweet chestnut
   purée de marron chestnut purée

marsala marsala wine

massepain marzipan

matelote fish stew

mauvais(e) bad

mayonnaise mayonnaise

médaillon medallion *[round piece of meat]*

mélanger; incorporer to blend; to mix

mélasse treacle

mélisse lemon balm

melon melon

menthe mint
   menthe poivrée peppermint
   menthe verte garden mint

menu menu

meringue meringue

merlan whiting

merlu *[colin]* hake

mérou grouper

meunière, à la covered with flour, fried in butter

miel honey
   rayon de miel, gaufre de miel honeycomb

mijoter to simmer

milanaise *[pasta]* with parmesan, tomato sauce; *[escalope]* breaded

millefeuille millefeuille, cream slice

minestrone minestrone (soup)

mirabelle (small) yellow plum

moelle bone marrow

mollusque mollusc

morilles morels

Mornay with white sauce, cheese, gratiné

morue cod

mouclade (cooked) mussels served with white sauce

moudre to grind

moule mussel
   moules marinière moules marinière *[cooked with white wine, onions, parsley]*

moulin à poivre pepper mill

moulu(e) ground (pepper, etc.)

mousse (de poisson, etc.) (fish, etc.) mousse
   mousse au chocolat chocolate mousse

moutarde mustard

moutarde de Meaux   whole grain mustard
mouton   mutton
muffin   muffin
mulet gris   grey mullet
mûr(e)   ripe
mûre (de ronce)   blackberry
mûre (du mûrier)   mulberry
myrtille   blueberry, blaeberry, whortleberry

Nn

nage, à la   (fish) served in its broth
Nantua   with crayfish
nappe   tablecloth
nature   plain (yoghurt, etc.); (tea, coffee) without milk
navarin   lamb stew
navet   turnip
navet, chou-navet   swede
nèfle   medlar
noisette   hazlenut, cobnut
noisette *[de viande]*   noisette *[small round piece of fillet or loin]*
noix   nut; walnut
   noix d'acajou; noix de cajou   cashew nut
   noix de coco   coconut
   noix de coco séchée   desiccated coconut
   noix muscade   nutmeg
   noix de pécan, noix de
   pacane   pecan nut
   noix du Brésil   brazil nut
   noix du noyer blanc
   d'Amérique   hickory nut
   noix du noyer de Queensland   macadamia nuts
noix de veau   tender cut of veal

non fumeurs *[section]*   non-smoking (area)
normande, à la   with cream, calvados or cider
nougatine   brittle
nouilles   noodles

Oo

oeuf   egg
   oeuf à la coque   soft-boiled egg
   oeuf dur   hard boiled egg
   oeuf mollet   soft boiled egg
   oeuf poché   poached egg
   oeuf pourri   bad egg
   oeuf sur le plat   fried egg
   oeufs à la neige *[île flottante]*   floating island
   oeufs et bacon, oeufs au bacon   bacon and eggs
   oeufs brouillés   scrambled eggs
   oeufs de cailles   quail's eggs
   oeufs de poisson; laitance   hard roe; soft roe
oie   goose
oignon   onion
olive   olive
   olives farcies   stuffed olives
   olives noires   black olives
   olives vertes   green olives
omble chevalier   char
omelette   omelette
   omelette au jambon   ham omelette
   omelette baveuse   omelette which is runny on top
   omelette norvégienne   baked alaska
orange   orange
   à l'orange   with orange

orge barley
   orge perlée pearl barley
origan oregano
ormeau abalone
ortie nettle
os bone
   os à moelle marrow bone
   (viande) avec l'os on the bone
oseille sorrel
ouvre-bouteille bottle opener

Pp

paille au fromage cheese straw
pain bread
   pain à la farine de maïs corn bread
   pain aux noix walnut bread
   pain blanc; pain de mie white loaf, white bread
   pain bis brown bread
   pain complet, pain de son wholemeal bread
   pain d'épice(s) gingerbread
   pain de seigle rye bread
   pain de viande meat loaf
   pain grec *[sans levain]* pitta bread
   pain grillé *[rôtie]* toast
   pain perdu, pain doré french toast
palourde, clovisse clam
pamplemousse grapefruit
   jus de pamplemousse grapefruit juice
panais parsnip
pané(e) breaded
papaye papaya, pawpaw
paprika paprika

parfait parfait
   parfait au café coffee parfait
Parmentier with potatoes
parmesan parmesan (cheese)
pastèque water melon
patate douce sweet potato; *[US]* yam
pâte pastry
   pâte à choux choux pastry
   pâte à frire batter
   pâte brisée shortcrust pastry
   pâte feuilletée puff pastry
pâte d'amandes almond paste
pâté pâté
   pâté de canard duck paté
   pâté de foie gras liver pâté
   pâté de soja quorn
pâté de gibier en croûte game pie
pâtes (alimentaires) pasta
   pâtes fraîches fresh pasta
pâtisserie French pastry; cake
patte leg
   pattes de dinde, de poulet drumsticks
paupiette thin rolled stuffed piece of meat
   paupiette de boeuf beef olive
   paupiette de veau veal olive
paysanne served with carrots, turnips, onions, celery, potatoes, bacon
peau, pelure skin; peel
pêche peach
peler, éplucher to peel
pelure, peau, écorce peel
   sans pelure, sans peau peeled
perche d'eau douce perch
perdrix; perdreau partridge; young partridge
périgourdine, à la with truffles, liver pâté
persil parsley
   persil frisé curly parsley
   persil plat flat parsley
pétillant(e) sparkling; fizzy
petit déjeuner breakfast

petit pain (bread) roll; bap
   petit pain au lait bun
petits fours petits fours
petits pois green peas, garden peas
   petits pois gourmands, pois mange-tout mangetout, sugar snap peas
pichet carafe
pickles pickles
pieds de porc pig's trotters
pigeon pigeon
pigeonneau squab
pilchard *[grosse sardine]* pilchard
piment doux *[poivron]* pepper, capsicum
   piment fort, piment rouge chili, red chilli, chili pepper
   piment (fort) en poudre chilli powder
   piment de la Jamaïque allspice
pimprenelle burnet
pintade guinea fowl, galeeny
piquant(e) hot *[strong]*
pistache pistachio (nut)
pistou (basil) pesto
plaquemine *[kaki]* persimmon
plat dish
   plat du jour plat du jour
   plat principal main course; *[US]* entree
plateau à fromage; plateau de fromages cheese board
pleurote oyster mushroom
poché(e) poached
   poché dans du lait poached in milk
pocher to poach
poêlé(e) pan-fried
point, à *[rose]* medium-rare
pointes d'asperges asparagus tips
poire pear
   poires au vin de Bourgogne pear poached in red wine
poireau leek
   petits poireaux baby leeks
pois pea

petits pois   green peas, garden peas
pois cassés   split peas
pois chiche   chickpea
pois gourmands, pois mange-tout, mangetouts
   mangetout
poisson   fish
poisson d'eau douce   freshwater fish, river fish
poisson de mer   sea fish
poisson frit   fried fish
poisson fumé   smoked fish
poisson plat   flat fish
poisson volant   flying fish
poisson-chat *[silure]*   catfish
poitrine   breast
poitrine d'agneau, de veau   breast of lamb, of veal
poitrine de boeuf   brisket of beef
poivre   pepper *[spice]*
moulin à poivre   pepper mill
poivre de cayenne   cayenne pepper
poivre en grains   whole pepper
poivre moulu   ground pepper
poivre noir, vert, blanc   black, green, white pepper
poivrière   pepper pot
poivron   pepper *[vegetable]*
poivron farci   stuffed pepper
poivron rouge *[piment doux]*   red pepper
poivron vert   green pepper
polenta *[semoule de maïs]*   polenta
pomme *[fruit]*   apple
pomme au four   baked apple
purée de pommes   apple puree
pomme (de terre)   potato
pomme de terre au four   baked potato
pommes (de terre) dauphine   mashed potatoes mixed with choux
pastry and fried
pommes (de terre) duchesse   duchesse potatoes
pommes de terre à l'anglaise, à l'eau   boiled potatoes
pommes de terre aux amandes   amandine potatoes
pommes de terre nouvelles   new potatoes
pommes de terre sautées   fried potoatoes

French-English

pommes allumettes matchstick potatoes
pommes chips (potato) crisps; *[US]* potato chips
pommes frites (potato) chips; *[US]* french fries
pommes purée mashed potatoes; *[US]* creamed potatoes

porc pork

pot jug

potage soup
potage au cari mulligatawny (soup)
potage aux légumes vegetable soup
potage St Germain green pea soup

potiron *[citrouille]* pumpkin

pouding pudding
pouding au riz; riz au lait *[cuit au four]* rice pudding
pouding cabinet cabinet pudding
pouding de Noël *[anglais]* Christmas pudding

poule boiling fowl

poulet chicken
poulet à la Kiev chicken kiev
poulet frit fried chicken
poulet rôti roast chicken

poulpe octopus

pourboire tip, gratuity

pourpier purslane

poussin poussin

poutassou blue whiting

pré-cuit(e); mi-cuit(e) par-boiled

prix price

profiteroles profiteroles

propre clean

provençale, à la with tomatoes, garlic, olive oil, olives

prune plum
prune de Damas damson

pruneau (sec) prune

prunelle sloe
eau de vie de prunelle sloe gin

purée puree
en purée mashed (potatoes); stewed (fruit)
purée de pois mushy peas
purée de pois cassés pease-pudding

purée de pommes   apple puree; apple sauce
purée de pommes de terre, pommes purée   mashed potatoes; *[US]* creamed potatoes

Qq

quark *[fromage blanc]*   quark
quenelle *[de brochet, de poulet ou veau]*   quenelle *[forcemeat of pike, chicken or veal, poached]*
queue de boeuf   oxtail
   soupe à la queue de boeuf   oxtail soup
queues de langoustine *[scampi]*   scampi
quiche   quiche
   quiche lorraine   quiche lorraine
   quiche au saumon fumé   smoked salmon quiche

Rr

râble (de lapin, lièvre)   saddle (of rabbit, of hare)
radis   radish, radishes
rafraîchi(e)   chilled
rafraîchisseur *[à vin]*   wine cooler
ragoût *[fricassée]*   stew
   ragoût de boeuf *[potée]*   hotpot
   ragoût de mouton à l'irlandaise   Irish stew
raie   skate
raifort   horseradish

French-English

raisin(s) *[de table]*   grape(s)
   raisins de Corinthe   currants
   raisins de Smyrne   sultanas
   raisins sec   raisins
ramequin *[met; plat]*   ramekin *[food; dish]*
rance   rancid
râpé(e)   grated
rascasse   redfish; rockfish
rassis(e)   stale
ratatouille   ratatouille
ravioli   ravioli
recette   recipe
réglisse   liquorice
reine-claude   greengage (plum)
requin   shark
rhubarbe   rhubarb
rhum   rum
ris de veau   sweetbreads
rissole   rissole
riz   rice
   riz au blanc, riz à la chinoise   boiled rice
   riz au lait au four, pouding
   au riz   baked rice, rice pudding
   riz complet   brown rice
   riz indien; riz Caroline   basmati rice
   riz pour risotto   risotto rice
   riz rond   pudding rice
   riz sauvage   wild rice
rognon   kidney
   rognons à la (sauce) diable   devilled kidneys
romaine *[laitue]*   romaine lettuce, cos lettuce
romarin   rosemary
romsteak   rump steak
roquette   rocket
rosbif   roast beef
rôti   roast
   rôti de boeuf *[rosbif]*   roast beef
   rôti de porc   roast pork
rôti(e)   roasted

rôtie *[pain grillé]*   toast
rôtir   to roast
rouget barbet   red mullet
rye *[whisky de seigle]*   rye whisky

Ss

sabayon   sabayon; syllabub
sablé   shortbread
saccharine   saccharin
safran   saffron
sagou   sago
saignant(e) *[viande]*   rare *[meat, steak]*
saindoux   lard
Saint Germain   with green peas
Saint-Pierre   dory, john dory
salade   salad; lettuce
   salade au poulet   chicken salad
   salade César   caesar salad
   salade composée, salade panachée   mixed salad
   salade de fruits   fruit salad
   salade de pommes de terre   potato salad
   salade de tomate   tomato salad
   salade verte   green salad
   salade Waldorf *[pommes, céleri, noix, avec mayonnaise]*   Waldorf
salad
sale   dirty *[plate, tablecloth, etc.]*
salé(e); avec sel   salted; salty
salir   to dirty
salsifis   salsify
sandre   pike-perch
sandwich   sandwich
   sandwich au jambon   ham sandwich

sanglier boar
sardine sardine
sarrasin *[blé noir]* buckwheat
sauce *[jus de viande]* sauce; gravy
sauce *[mayonnaise; vinaigrette]* dressing
sauce sauce
   sauce à l'aneth dill sauce
   sauce à la crème cream sauce
   sauce à la menthe (fraîche) mint sauce
   sauce au beurre butter sauce
   sauce au chocolat chocolate sauce
   sauce au pain bread sauce
   sauce aux canneberges cranberry sauce
   sauce bigarade *[bitter]* orange sauce
   sauce blanche *[béchamel]* white sauce
   sauce béarnaise béarnaise (sauce)
   sauce bordelaise bordelaise sauce
   sauce diable devilled sauce
   sauce espagnole brown sauce
   sauce hollandaise hollandaise sauce
   sauce madère madeira sauce
   sauce Mornay cheese sauce
   sauce soja soy sauce, soya sauce
   sauce tartare tartar(e) sauce
   sauce tomate tomato sauce
saucisse sausage
saucisson French sausage
   saucisson italien salami
sauge sage
saumon salmon
   saumon fumé smoked salmon
   darne de saumon salmon steak
sauté(e) sautéed
sauter à la chinoise stir-fry
saxifrage saxifrage
seau de glace bucket of ice
sec (sèche); séché(e) dry; dried
   très sec very dry (wine)
seiche cuttlefish

seigle rye

sel salt
   qui contient peu de sel low-salt (dish)
   sel gemme rock salt

selle (d'agneau) saddle

semoule semolina

serveuse waitress

service service
   service compris service included
   service non compris service not included
   service à la discrétion du
   client service: discretionary

serviette (de table) napkin, serviette

silure *[poisson chat]* catfish

sirop syrup
   sirop de maïs corn syrup
   sirop d'érable maple syrup

soja (fève de) soy bean, soya bean, soja bean
   sauce soja soy sauce, soya sauce

sole Dover sole; sand sole

sommelier wine waiter

son (de blé) bran

sorbet; granité sherbet; sorbet

sorgho sorghum

Soubise with onions

soucoupe saucer

soufflé soufflé
   soufflé au fromage cheese soufflé
   soufflé aux fraises strawberry soufflé

soupe soup
   soupe à la queue de boeuf oxtail soup
   soupe à l'oignon onion soup
   soupe aux légumes vegetable soup
   soupe aux pois (cassés) pea soup *[with split peas]*
   soupe de poisson(s) fish soup
   soupe de poulet chicken soup
   soupe de poulet et poireaux cock-a-leekie (soup) *[chicken and leeks]*

souris d'agneau knuckle-end of leg of lamb (on the bone)

spaghetti spaghetti
sprat *[harenguet]* sprat
steak steak
   steak au poivre pepper steak
   steak et frites steak and chips
   steak tartare raw minced fillet steak served with raw egg yolk, capers, onions
stout *[bière brune]* stout
strudel aux pommes apple strudel
succédané de lait *[en poudre]* coffee whitener
sucre sugar
   sucre de canne cane sugar
   sucre d'érable maple sugar
   sucre d'orge barley sugar
   sucre glace, sucre en poudre icing sugar
   sucre roux *[cassonade]* (soft) brown sugar
   sucre semoule caster sugar
   sucre vanillé vanilla sugar
sucré(e) sweet
suif (de boeuf) suet
suprême de poulet *[blanc, filet]* chicken breast, breast of chicken
surgelé(e) frozen
syllabub *[sabayon]* syllabub

Tt

table table
tagliatelle tagliatelle
tamiser to sift
tanche tench
tangerine tangerine
tapioca tapioca
tarte pie

part de tarte   slice of pie
tarte aux noix de pécan   pecan pie
tarte aux pommes   apple pie
tarte Tatin   upside down apple pie *[apples covered with pastry served upside down]*

tartelette   (small) tart
tartelette à la crème   custard tart
tartelette aux pommes   apple tart

tasse   cup
tasse à café   coffee cup
tasse à thé   tea cup
tasse de café; un café   cup of coffee
tasse de chocolat   cup of coacoa, of hot chocolate
tasse de thé; un thé   cup of tea
tasse et soucoupe   cup and saucer

tendre *[viande]*   tender

terrine   terrine

thé   tea
thé (au) citron   lemon tea
thé au lait   tea with milk
thé de Chine   china tea
thé glacé   iced tea
thé japonais   japan tea
thé nature   tea without milk or sugar

théière   teapot

thon   tuna, tunny
thon blanc   albacore (tuna)

thym   thyme

timbale de poisson   fisherman's pie

tire-bouchon   corkscrew

tisane   herbal tea

tofu *[pâté de soja]*   tofu

toilettes, wc, lavabo   lavatory, toilet

tomate   tomato
tomate oblongue, allongée   plum tomato
tomates séchées (au soleil)   sun-dried tomatoes

topinambour   jerusalem artichoke

tournedos   fillet steak

tournesol   sunflower

graines de tournesol   sunflower seeds
huile de tournesol   sunflower oil
tourte *[pie de viande]*   meat pie
tourteau *[crabe]*   crab
tranche   slice
tranche de jambon   slice of ham
tranche de pain   slice of bread
tranche napolitaine   neapolitan ice-cream
tranché(e)   sliced (bread, etc.)
travers de porc   spare ribs
tremper   to dip
trévise *[chicorée rouge]*   radicchio
tripes   tripe
tripes à la mode de Caen   tripe cooked with vegetables and white wine, for 7 to 8 hours
truffe   truffle
truffe au chocolat   chocolate truffle
truite   trout
truite arc-en-ciel   rainbow trout
truite saumonée; truite de mer   salmon trout, sea trout
turbot   turbot

Vv

vaisselle *[service de porcelaine]*   china (service)
vanille   vanilla
extrait de vanille   vanilla essence
glace à la vanille   vanilla ice cream
veau *[animal]*   calf
veau *[viande]*   veal
escalope de veau   veal escalope
foie de veau   calf's liver
noix de veau   tender cut of veal

végétarien (-ienne)   vegetarian
velouté (de)   cream (of) *[soup]*
venaison   venison
vermicelle   vermicelli
verre   glass
   verre à eau   glass for water
   verre à vin   wine glass
   verre d'eau   glass of water
   verre de vin   glass of wine
   verre propre   clean glass
viande   meat
   viande de cheval   horse meat
   viande en cocotte   pot roast
   viande froide   cold meat
   viande fumé   smoked meat
vichyssoise   vichyssoise
vin   wine
   vin blanc   white wine
   vin corsé   full-bodied wine
   vin de Bordeaux   Bordeaux wine
   vin de Bourgogne   Burgundy (wine)
   vin de Porto   port
   vin de table   table wine
   vin doux, vin de dessert   dessert wine, sweet wine
   vin léger   light-bodied wine
   vin local; vin de pays   local wine
   vin (de la) maison   house wine
   vin mousseux; vin pétillant   sparkling wine
   vin rosé   rosé (wine)
   vin rouge   red wine
   vin sec   dry wine
vinaigre   vinegar
   vinaigre balsamique   balsamic vinegar
   vinaigre de cidre   cider vinegar
   vinaigre de vin (rouge, blanc)   wine vinegar
vinaigrette   french dressing, vinaigrette
volaille   fowl; chicken
vol-au-vent   *[bouchée feuilletée; timbale]*   vol au vent

Ww Xx Yy Zz

WC   toilet, lavatory
whiskey irlandais   Irish whiskey
whisky écossais   whisky
xérès   sherry
yaourt, yogourt   yoghurt
   yaourt à la grecque   greek yoghurt
   yaourt nature   plain yoghurt
   yaourt aux myrtilles   blueberry yoghurt
zabaglione   zabaglione
zeste *[écorce râpée]*   zest
   zeste de citron   lemon zest, grated lemon peel

English-French

Aa

abalone ormeau
absinthe absinthe
account compte
aïloli sauce ailloli, aïoli
albacore (tuna) thon blanc, germon
ale bière (anglaise) blonde; *see also* **beer**
alfalfa sprouts germes de luzerne
allspice piment de la Jamaïque
almond amande douce
   almond paste pâte d'amandes
   with almonds aux amandes
amandine potatoes pommes de terre aux amandes
anchovy anchois
   anchovy butter beurre d'anchois
   anchovy paste purée, pâte d'anchois
angel (food) cake angel cake *[génoise sans jaune d'oeufs]*
angel fish ange de mer
angel hair pasta cheveux d'ange
angels on horseback angels on horseback *[huîtres entourées de bacon, grillées, sur toast]*
angelica angélique
angler baudroie, lotte (de mer)
aniseed anis
aperitif apéritif
appetizer (drink or food) *[US]*
   see **starter course** apéritif; amuse-gueule; hors-d'oeuvres
apple pomme *[fruit]*
   apple fritter beignet de pommes
   apple juice jus de pomme
   apple pie tarte aux pommes
   apple puree purée de pommes
   apple sauce purée de pommes *[peu sucrée]*
   apple strudel strudel aux pommes

apple turnover   chausson aux pommes
apple tart   tartelette aux pommes
baked apple   pomme au four
apricot   abricot
aroma   arôme; bouquet (d'un vin)
arrowroot   arrow-root
artichoke   artichaut
ashtray   cendrier
asparagus   asperge
   asparagus tips   pointes d'asperges
aspic   aspic
assorted vegetables   choix de légumes, légumes variés
aubergine, eggplant   aubergine
au gratin *[US]*   gratiné(e), au gratin
avocado   avocat

Bb

baby corn (cob)   tout petit épi de maïs
baby leeks   petits poireaux
bacon   bacon; lard fumé
   bacon and eggs   oeufs au bacon
bad   mauvais(e)
   bad egg   oeuf pourri
bake   (faire) cuire au four
baked   cuit(e) au four
   baked alaska   omelette norvégienne
   baked apple   pomme au four
   baked beans   haricots blancs aux tomates; fèves au lard
   baked custard   flan
   baked potato   pomme de terre au four
   baked rice, rice pudding   riz au lait au four, pouding au riz
bakery   boulangerie

balsamic vinegar vinaigre balsamique
banana banane
   banana fritter beignet de bananes
   banana split banana split *[banane, glace à la vanille, Chantilly, amandes]*
   banana flambé bananes flambées
barbecue barbecue
barbecued grillé(e) au barbecue
barbel/red mullet rouget barbet
barley orge
   barley sugar sucre d'orge
   barley water sirop d'orgeat *[fait avec de l'orge]*
basil basilic
   basil pesto pistou
basmati rice riz indien; riz Caroline
bass, sea bass loup (de mer), bar
batter pâte à frire
bavarian cream bavarois
bay leaf feuille de laurier
bean haricot
   bean sprouts germes de soja
   broad bean grosse fève; fève des marais
   french bean, green bean, string bean haricot vert
   kidney bean, red bean haricot rouge
   runner beans haricots grimpants
   soja bean (fève de) soja
béarnaise (sauce) sauce béarnaise
béchamel (sauce) (sauce) béchamel
beech nuts faînes
beef boeuf
   beefsteak *[US]* bifteck, steak
   beef tea bouillon de boeuf
   beef Wellington filet de boeuf en croûte
   roast beef rosbif
beer bière
   draught beer bière (à la) pression
beetroot betterave
bergamot bergamote

bib (child's) bavette, bavoir

bilberry airelle, myrtille

bill, [US] check addition

biscuit, [US] cookies biscuits, gâteaux secs

biscuit [US] petit pain *[qui ressemble au scone anglais]*

bitter amer (amère)

bitter (beer) bière anglaise pression

black beans haricots noirs

blackberry mûre (de ronce)

black cherry cerise noire

black coffee café noir

blackcurrant cassis *[groseille noire]*

black forest cake/gateau forêt-noire

black halibut flétan noir

black pepper poivre noir

black pudding boudin noir

blaeberry airelle, myrtille

blanch blanchir

blancmange blanc-manger

blend mélanger; incorporer

blinis blinis

bloater hareng bouffi

blueberry myrtille, bleuet

blue cheese fromage bleu

blue whiting poutassou

boar sanglier; *[jeune]* marcassin

bogue [fish] bogue

boil (faire) bouillir

boiled bouilli(e), cuit(e) à l'eau, à l'anglaise

    boiled egg oeuf à la coque

    boiled ham jambon poché

    boiled potatoes pommes de terre à l'anglaise, à l'eau

    boiled rice riz au blanc, riz à la chinoise

    hard boiled egg oeuf dur

bombe bombe

bone os

    boned désossé(e) *[viande, poisson]*

on the bone   *[viande]* avec l'os; *[poisson]* dont les arêtes n'ont pas été retirées

bones (of fish)   arêtes (de poisson)

bonito   bonite

borage   bourrache

bordelaise sauce   sauce bordelaise

borlotti beans   haricots italiens

bouquet garni   bouquet garni

bottle   bouteille

    bottle opener   ouvre-bouteille

bowl   bol

brains   cervelle (de veau)

braise *[verb]*   braiser

braised   braisé(e)

bran   son (de blé)

brandy   cognac

    cherry brandy   cherry brandy, liqueur de cerise

brawn   fromage de tête

brazil nut   noix du Brésil

bread   pain

    breadcrumbs   chapelure

    bread knife   petit couteau *[pour beurrer son pain]*

    brown bread   pain complet

    bread sauce   sauce au pain

breaded   pané(e)

breakfast   petit déjeuner

bream, sea bream   brème (de mer)

breast   poitrine

    breast of lamb, veal   poitrine d'agneau, de veau

    chicken breast   suprême de poulet

brill   barbue

brioche   brioche

brisket (of beef)   poitrine (de boeuf)

brittle   nougatine

broad bean   grosse fève; fève des marais

broccoli   (chou) brocoli

broth   bouillon

brown *[verb]*   (faire) brunir; (faire) dorer

brown bread   pain complet
brown butter   beurre noisette
brown rice   riz complet
brown sugar   sucre roux, cassonade
brown sauce   sauce espagnole
brussels sprouts   choux de Bruxelles
bubble and squeak   choux et pommes de terre frits
buckwheat   sarrasin, blé noir
buffet   buffet
bulgar wheat, bulgur wheat   blé concassé
bun   petit pain au lait
burbot   lotte (d'eau douce)
burdock   glouteron, bardane
burgundy (wine)   (vin de) bourgogne; *see also* **wine**
burnet   pimprenelle
burnt   brûlé(e)
butter   beurre
   butterfish   blennie
   buttermilk   lait de beurre, babeurre
   butter sauce   sauce au beurre
   with butter   avec beurre; au beurre
   without butter   sans beurre

Cc

cabbage   chou
cabinet pudding   pouding cabinet
caesar salad   salade César
caffeine   caféine
   caffeine-free / decaffeinated   sans caféine; décaféiné(e)
cake   gâteau
   carrot cake   gâteau aux carottes

cream cake gâteau à la crème
fruit cake cake *[aux fruits confits]*
sponge cake génoise
calf veau
   calf's brains cervelle de veau
   calf's liver foie de veau
camomile camomille
canapés canapés
candied confit(e)
   candied peel zeste confit, écorce confite
candle chandelle
candlestick chandelier
candy *[US]* bonbon
cane sugar sucre de canne
canned *[US]* en boîte (de conserve)
cantaloup (melon) cantaloup
capers câpres
capon chapon
capsicum piment doux, poivron
carafe carafe
caramel caramel
caraway (seeds) cumin des prés, carvi
carbohydrate glucides *[hydrates de carbone]*
cardamom cardamome
carp carpe
carrot carotte
   carrot cake gâteau aux carottes
carve découper
cassata cassate
cashew nut noix d'acajou; noix de cajou
casserole casserole
caster sugar sucre semoule
castor broth bouillon de légumes
catfish poisson-chat, silure
catsup, *[US]* **ketchup** ketchup, sauce tomate
cauliflower chou-fleur
   cauliflower cheese chou-fleur sauce Mornay, au gratin
caviar caviar

cayenne pepper   poivre de cayenne
celeriac   céleri-rave
celery   céleri
cereal (breakfast)   céréales
chair   chaise
champagne   champagne
chantilly   (crème) Chantilly
chanterelle   chanterelle
char   omble chevalier
charcoal   charbon de bois
  charcoal-grilled   grillé(e) au charbon de bois
chard   bette, blette
charlotte   charlotte
  apple charlotte   charlotte aux pommes
cheddar (cheese)   (fromage) cheddar
cheese   fromage
  cheddar (cheese)   (fromage) cheddar
  cheese board   plateau à fromage; plateau de fromages
  cheesecake   gâteau au fromage blanc
  cream cheese   fromage à la crème
  cheese sauce   sauce Mornay
  cheese soufflé   soufflé au fromage
  cheese straw   paille, allumette au fromage
cherry   cerise
  cherry brandy   cherry brandy, liqueur de cerise
chervil   cerfeuil
chestnut (sweet)   marron; châtaigne
  sweet chestnut   châtaigne; marron
  water chestnut   châtaigne d'eau
chickpea   pois chiche
chicken   poulet
  roast chicken   poulet rôti
  breast of chicken   suprême de poulet
  chicken gumbo   (potage de) poulet et gombo
  chicken kiev   poulet à la Kiev
  chicken livers   foies de poulets
  chicken salad   salade au poulet
  chicken soup   soupe de poulet
chicory   endive

chilled rafraîchi(e)

chilli piment fort; piment rouge
   chilli-con-carne chili con carne
   chilli pepper piment fort; piment rouge
   chilli powder piment en poudre

china (service) vaisselle; service de porcelaine

china tea thé de Chine

chinese cabbage chou de Chine

chipped (glass, plate) (verre, assiette) ébréché(e)

chips (pommes) frites

chips *[US]* (pommes) chips

chitterling *[US]* friture de tripes *[découpées en morceaux]*

chives ciboulette; civette

chocolate chocolat
   chocolate eclair éclair au chocolat
   chocolate mousse mousse au chocolat
   chocolate sauce sauce au chocolat
   chocolate truffle truffe au chocolat

chop (cutlet) côte; côtelette

chopped (into pieces) en dés; (persil) haché

chopsticks baguettes

choux pastry pâte à choux

chowder *[US]* soupe de poisson à base de lait

Christmas cake gâteau de Noël *[anglais]*

Christmas log bûche de Noël

Christmas pudding pouding de Noël *[anglais]*

cider cidre
   cider vinegar vinaigre de cidre

cinnamon cannelle

citron cédrat

clam clam; palourde
   clam chowder chowder aux palourdes

claret bordeaux rouge; *see also* **red wine**

clean propre

clear up desservir (la table)

clear soup consommé

clementine clémentine

clove clou de girofle

cobnut   noisette

cock-a-leekie (soup)   soupe de poulet et poireaux

cockles   coques

cocoa   (poudre de) cacao
   cocoa butter   beurre de cacao
   cup of cocoa   une tasse de cacao, de chocolat

coconut   noix de coco
   coconut milk   lait de coco
   desiccated coconut   noix de coco séchée

cod   morue, cabillaud

coffee   café
   cappucino coffee   cappucino
   coffee whitener   succédané de lait *[en poudre]*
   coffee parfait   parfait au café
   coffee pot   cafetière
   coffee spoon   cuillère à café
   decaffeinated coffee   café décaféiné; un déca
   espresso / expresso coffee   café express
   filter coffee   café filtre
   instant coffee   café soluble
   latte coffee   café au lait

cold   froid(e)
   cold cuts *[US]*   assiette de viandes froides, assiette anglaise
   cold meat   viande froide

coley *[coalfish]*   lieu noir, colin

collared beef   rosbif roulé *[ficelé]*

condensed milk   lait condensé

condiment   condiment

confectioner's cream   crème pâtissière

conger eel   congre, anguille de mer

consommé (soup)   consommé
   cold consommé   consommé froid; consommé en gelée

continental breakfast   café complet

cook, chef   chef

cookies *[US]*   biscuits, gâteaux secs

coriander   coriandre

corkscrew   tire-bouchon

corn   maïs
   corn bread   pain à la farine de maïs

English-French

cornflour fécule de maïs

corn on the cob épi de maïs, maïs en épi

corn syrup sirop de maïs

sweetcorn maïs (en épi, en grains)

corned beef boeuf de conserve

cornet (ice cream) cornet (de glace)

cos lettuce (laitue) romaine

cottage cheese fromage 'cottage'

courgette courgette

couscous couscous

crab crabe, tourteau, dormeur

dressed crab crabe froid à l'anglaise, à la russe

prepared crab crabe décortiqué

crackling couenne croquante (du rôti de porc)

cranberry canneberge

cranberry sauce sauce de canneberges

crawfish langouste

crayfish écrevisse

cream crème

double cream crème épaisse

single cream crème légère

whipped cream crème Chantilly, crème fouettée

cream cheese fromage à la crème

cream cake gâteau à la crème

cream sauce sauce à la crème *[béchamel]*

cream slice millefeuille *[où la crème Chantilly remplace la crème pâtissière]*

cream tea thé accompagné de scones avec confiture et crème fraîche

cream of crème (de), velouté (de)

cream of asparagus soup crème d'asperges

cream of chicken soup crème de volaille; velouté de volaille

cream of tomato soup crème de tomates

creamed en purée; à la crème

creamed potato *[US]* purée de pommes de terre

creamed spinach purée d'épinards à la crème

creamy en crème; crémeux(-euse), velouté(e)

crème caramel *[baked custard]* crème caramel

crème fraîche crème fraîche

cress cresson
crispbread biscotte
crisps (pommes) chips
croquette potatoes croquettes de pommes de terre
croutons croûtons
crumble crumble
crumpet petite crêpe épaisse *[non sucrée]*
crystallised fruit fruits confits
cucumber concombre
  cucumber sandwich sandwich au concombre
cumin (seed) cumin
cup tasse
  cup and saucer tasse et soucoupe
  cup of coffee tasse de café; un café
  cup of tea tasse de thé; un thé
  coffee cup tasse à café
  tea cup tasse à thé
cured fumé(e); mariné(e); salé(e)
currants raisins de Corinthe
curry curry, cari
custard crème anglaise
  baked custard flan
  custard apple anone, pomme canelle
  custard sauce crème anglaise
  custard tart tartelette à la crème
cutlery couvert
cutlet côtelette
cuttlefish seiche

English-French

Dd

dab limande
damson prune de Damas

date datte

date plum kaki

debone/fillet (verb) désosser; lever les filets

decaffeinated/decaf (café) décaféiné; un déca

deep-fried cuit(e) à grande friture

deer/venison chevreuil

defrost dégeler

delicious délicieux (-euse)

demerara sugar sucre roux cristallisé

dessert dessert

   dessert wine vin doux, vin de dessert

devilled (à la) diable

   devilled kidneys rognons à la (sauce) diable

   devilled sauce sauce (à la) diable

diced (cubed) en cube

dill aneth

   dill sauce sauce à l'aneth

dinner dîner

dip *[verb]* tremper

dirty *[adj]* sale

dirty *[verb]* salir

dish plat

dog fish aiguillat, chien de mer

done cuit(e)

   under-done pas assez cuit(e); *[viande]* saignant(e)

   well-done bien cuit(e)

dory, john dory Saint-Pierre, dorée

doughnut beignet

   jam doughnut beignet fourré à la confiture

dover sole sole

draught beer bière (à la) pression

dressing sauce; mayonnaise; vinaigrette

dried séché(e); sec (sèche)

   sun-dried (tomatoes) tomates séchées (au soleil)

drumsticks pattes de dinde ou de poulet

dry (wine) (vin) sec

Dublin bay prawn langoustine

duchesse potatoes pommes (de terre) duchesse

duck (domestic) canard (domestique)
duck (wild) canard sauvage
  duck paté pâté de canard
  duck with oranges canard à l'orange
  duckling caneton
dumpling boulette de pâte
  potato dumpling gnocchi Parmentier

Ee

éclair éclair
eel anguille
egg oeuf
  boiled egg oeuf à la coque
  egg and bacon oeuf et bacon
  egg cup coquetier
  egg white blanc d'oeuf
  egg yolk jaune d'oeuf
  fried egg oeuf sur le plat
  hard boiled egg oeuf dur
  omelette omelette
  poached egg oeuf poché
  scrambled eggs oeufs brouillés
  soft boiled egg oeuf mollet
eggplant/aubergine aubergine
elderberry baie de sureau
endive chicorée frisée
entree entrée
entree [US] [main course] plat principal
escalope escalope
  turkey escalope escalope de dinde
  veal escalope escalope de veau
essence extrait (de)

ewe's milk lait de brebis
ewe's milk cheese fromage de (lait de) brebis

Ff

faggot ballottine
farm (eggs, chickens) (oeufs, poulets) fermiers
fat *[adj]* gras (grasse)
fat *[noun]* gras
   fat-free sans gras
fennel fenouil
feta cheese (fromage) feta, féta
fig figue
filbert aveline
fillet filet
   fillet steak tournedos, steak prélevé dans le filet
   fillet of beef filet de boeuf
filleted désossé(e); en filets
filo pastry pâte (à pâtisserie) très mince
filter coffee café filtre
fine beans haricots verts (fins)
fish poisson
   anchovy anchois
   angel fish ange de mer
   bass, sea bass loup (de mer), bar
   bloater hareng bouffi
   bream brème
   brill barbue
   burbot lotte (d'eau douce)
   catfish poisson-chat, silure
   cod morue, cabillaud
   coley *[coalfish]* colin, lieu noir
   conger eel congre, anguille de mer

crayfish   écrevisse
cuttlefish   seiche
dog fish   aiguillat, chien de mer
dory, john dory   Saint-Pierre, dorée
dover sole   sole *[la vraie]*
eel   anguille
fish and chips   friture de poisson avec frites
fish stew   matelote; bouillabaisse
fish soup   soupe de poissons
fish cake   croquette de poisson
flounder   flet
flying fish   poisson volant
grey mullet   mulet gris
haddock   aiglefin, églefin
hake   merlu, colin
halibut   flétan
herring   hareng
kipper   hareng saur, fumé
lemon sole   limande-sole
mackerel   maquereau
monkfish   baudroie, lotte de mer
pike   brochet
pike-perch   sandre
pilchard   pilchard, (grosse) sardine
redfish   rascasse
red mullet   rouget barbet
rockfish   rascasse
roe   oeufs de poisson; laitance
sea bass   loup (de mer), bar
sea bream   brème de mer
sea trout   truite de mer; truite saumonée
shark   requin; aiguillat
skate   raie
skipjack   bonite
smelt   éperlan
sole   sole
sturgeon   esturgeon
swordfish   espadon
tench   tanche
trout   truite
tunny, tuna   thon

    turbot turbot
    whitebait *[sprats]* blanchaille
    whiting merlan
fisherman's pie timbale de poisson
fizzy pétillant(e); gazeux(-euse)
flageolet (beans) flageolet
flakes flocons
flambé flambé(e)
flan flan
flat fish poisson plat
floating island(s) oeufs à la neige, île(s) flottante(s)
flounder flet
flour farine
flying fish poisson volant
fondant fondant
fondue fondue
fool mousse faite de fruits. crème anglaise et Chantilly
fork fourchette
fowl volaille
    boiling fowl poule
free-range (oeuf, poulet) fermier
french beans haricots verts
french dressing vinaigrette
french fries *[US]* (pommes) frites
french toast pain perdu, pain doré
fresh frais (fraîche)
freshwater (fish) (poisson) d'eau douce
fried frit(e)
fried chicken poulet frit
fried egg oeuf sur le plat
fried fish poisson frit
    mixed fried fish friture de poissons
frisée (salad) chicorée frisée
fritter beignet
    apple fritter beignet de pommes
frog's legs cuisses de grenouilles
frozen surgelé(e)
fruit fruit

fruit cocktail   salade de fruits, macédoine de fruits
fruit juice   jus de fruits
fruit salad   salade de fruits, macédoine de fruits
fry   frire
fudge   fondant au chocolat
full-bodied wine   vin corsé
full-cream milk   lait entier
full-fat (cheese)   (fromage) de lait entier

Gg

galantine   galantine
galeeny   pintade
game   gibier (à plume; à poil); chevreuil
   game pie   pâté de gibier en croûte
gammon   jambon fumé (désossé)
garden mint   menthe verte
garden peas   petits pois frais
garlic   ail
garlicky   aillé(e)
gateau   gâteau
gazpacho   gaspacho
gelatine   gélatine
ghee   beurre clarifié *[cuisine Indienne]*
gherkin   cornichon
giblets   abats; *[de volaille]* abattis
gin   genièvre
ginger   gingembre
   ginger beer   bière au gingembre
   gingerbread   pain d'épice(s)
   ginger cake   gâteau au gingembre
glacé cherry   cerise confite

glass verre
  clean glass verre propre
  glass of water verre d'eau
  wine glass verre à vin
glazed glacé(e)
goat chèvre
  goat's cheese fromage de chèvre
  goat's milk lait de chèvre
goose oie
  goose liver foie d'oie
gooseberry groseille à maquereau
goulash goulash, goulasch
granita granité
granulated sugar sucre granulé
grape(s) raisin(s) (de table)
grapefruit pamplemousse
grated râpé(e)
gratuity pourboire
gravy sauce; jus de viande
  gravy boat saucière
greek yoghurt yaourt à la grecque *[au lait de brebis]*
green beans haricots verts
green olives olives vertes
green peas petits pois
green pepper poivron vert
green salad salade verte
greengage (plum) reine-claude
greenland halibut flétan noir
greens légumes verts
grenadine grenadine
grey mullet mulet gris
grill *[verb]* griller, cuire sur le gril
grill *[noun]* gril
  mixed grill assiette de viandes grillées (assorties)
grilled grillé(e)
grind moudre
gristle cartilage, croquant
grits *[US]* bouillie de maïs; gruau de maïs

groats gruau d'avoine
ground moulu(e); haché(e)
   ground beef hachis, boeuf haché
groundnut oil huile d'arachide
grouper mérou
grouse grouse
guava goyave
gudgeon goujon
guinea fowl pintade
gumbo gombo
gurnard grondin

Hh

haddock aiglefin, églefin
haggis haggis *[estomac de mouton contenant un hachis d'abattis de mouton, oignons et avoine, le tout bouilli]*
hake merlu, colin
halibut flétan
ham jambon
   boiled ham jambon poché
hamburger hamburger
hard boiled egg oeuf dur
hard cheese fromage à pâte dure
hard roe oeufs de poisson
hare lièvre
haricot beans haricots blancs
hash browns *[US]* pommes de terre en dés, avec oignons, sautées
hazelnut noisette; aveline
heart coeur
heat up chauffer; réchauffer
herbs fines herbes

herbal tea tisane; infusion
herring hareng
hickory nut noix du noyer blanc d'Amérique
hollandaise sauce sauce hollandaise
hominy grits *[US]* bouillie de maïs
honey miel
honeycomb rayon de miel, gaufre de miel
honeydew melon cavaillon
hors d'oeuvre hors d'oeuvre
horse mackerel chinchard
horse meat viande de cheval
horseradish raifort
hot *[not cold]* *chaud(e);* *[strong]* piquant(e)
hot dog hot dog *[saucisse de Francfort dans un petit pain]*
hotpot ragoût (de boeuf), potée

Ii

ice glace
   bucket of ice seau de glace *[pour garder le vin frais]*
ice cream glace, crème glacée
   ice cream cone cornet de glace, de crème glacée
   ice cream scoop boule de glace, de crème glacée
ice cube glaçon
ice lolly esquimau
iceberg lettuce laitue iceberg
icing glace, glaçage
   icing sugar sucre glace, en poudre
ide (fish) ide
ingredients ingrédients, éléments
instant coffee café soluble
Irish stew ragoût de mouton à l'irlandaise
Irish whiskey whiskey irlandais

Jj

jam   confiture
japan tea   thé japonais
jelly (savoury)   aspic, chaud-froid, galantine
jelly (sweet/pudding)   gelée; fruits en gelée
jelly [US] [jam]   confiture
jello [US]   gelée *[parfumée à la fraise, etc.]*
jerusalem artichoke   topinambour
john dory, dory   Saint-Pierre, dorée
jug   pot
jugged hare   civet de lièvre
juice   jus (de fruits; de viande)
julienne   julienne

Kk

kaki   kaki, plaquemine
kale   chou vert frisé *[non pommé]*
kebab   kébab, brochette (de viande)
kedgeree   riz au poisson fumé avec oeufs durs et cari
ketchup   ketchup
key lime pie   tarte à la crème de citron vert
kidney   rognon
kidney beans   haricots rouges
king prawn   crevette rose
kipper   hareng fumé, hareng saur
kiwi fruit   kiwi

knife couteau
knuckle jarret
kohlrabi chou-rave
kosher casher, kasher
kumquat kumquat

LI

ladies fingers gombos
lager bière blonde
lamb agneau
   lamb chop côtelette d'agneau
lamb's lettuce mâche
langoustine langoustine
lard saindoux
lark alouette
lasagne lasagne
lavatory toilettes, wc, lavabo
lavender lavande
leek poireau
leg patte
   leg of lamb gigot d'agneau
legumes légumineuse
lemon citron
   lemon balm mélisse
   lemon grass citronnelle
   lemon juice jus de citron
   lemon sole limande-sole
   lemon zest zeste, écorce de citron
   lemonade limonade; citron pressé
lentil lentille
lettuce laitue, salade

lime   citron vert, lime
ling   lingue
light-bodied wine   vin léger
liqueur   liqueur
liquorice   réglisse
liver   foie
   liver sausage   leberwurst
loaf   pain
   meat loaf   pain de viande
   white loaf   pain blanc; pain de mie
lobster   homard
   lobster bisque   bisque de homard
loganberry   loganberry
loin (of veal, pork, venison)   longe (de veau, porc, chevreuil)
low-fat (diet)   (régime) basses calories
low in fat   qui contient peu de gras; basses calories
low-salt   qui contient peu de sel; hyposodé(e)
lunch   déjeuner; lunch
luncheon meat   viande froide pressée *[de conserve]*
lychee   litchi, letchi
lythe   lieu jaune

Mm

macadamia nuts   noix du noyer de Queensland
macaroni   macaroni
macaroon   macaron
mace   macis
mackerel   maquereau
madeira   madère
   madeira cake   génoise au citron; gâteau de Savoie
   madeira sauce   sauce madère

maids of honour   tartelette à la frangipane (de Richmond)
maize   maïs
malt   malt
mandarin   mandarine
mangetout   pois gourmands, pois mange-tout, mangetouts
mango   mangue
mangosteen   mangouste, mangoustan
maple syrup   sirop d'érable
maple sugar   sucre d'érable
margarine   margarine
marinated   mariné(e)
marjoram   marjolaine
market   marché
marmalade   marmelade d'oranges, confiture d'oranges
marrow (vegetable)   courge
marrow bone   os à moelle
   bone marrow   moelle
marsala wine   marsala
marshmallow   guimauve
marzipan   massepain
mashed   en purée
mashed potatoes   pommes purée
matches   allumettes
matchstick potatoes   pommes allumettes
mayonnaise   mayonnaise
mead   hydromel
meat   viande
   meat ball   boulette de viande
   meat loaf   terrine; pain de viande
   meat pie   tourte; pie de viande
   medium-rare   à point, rose
   rare   saignant; bleu
   well done   bien cuit
medallion   médaillon
medlar   nèfle
melon   melon
melted butter   beurre fondu
menu   menu

meringue   meringue

milk   lait

   (cow's) milk   lait de vache

   (ewe's) milk   lait de brebis

   (goat's) milk   lait de chèvre

   milk chocolate   chocolat au lait

   poached in milk   poché dans du lait

   with milk   avec (du) lait; au lait

   without milk   sans lait

minced meat   hachis, viande hachée

mincemeat   mincemeat *[préparation sucrée à base d'un mélange de fruits et raisins secs, et de suif]*

mince pie   mince pie *[tarte(lette) avec mincemeat]*

mineral water   eau minérale

   fizzy mineral water   eau gazeuse

   still mineral water   eau plate

minestrone (soup)   (soupe) minestrone

mint   menthe

   mint sauce   sauce à la menthe (fraîche)

   mint jelly   gelée à la menthe

mixed grill   assiette de viandes grillées (assorties)

mixed salad   salade composée

mixed vegetables   macédoine de légumes

mollusc   mollusque; fruits de mer

monkfish   baudroie, lotte de mer

morels   morilles

muffin *[UK]*   muffin *[petit pain]*

muffin *[US]*   muffin *[petit gâteau avec bleuets, etc.]*

mug   mug, tasse *[sans soucoupe]*

mulberry   mûre *[du mûrier]*

mullet   rouget

mulligatawny (soup)   potage au cari

mushroom   champignon

   button mushrooms   champignons de Paris

mushy peas   purée de pois

mussel   moule

mustard   moutarde

mutton   mouton

Nn

napkin serviette (de table)
natural nature
neapolitan ice-cream tranche napolitaine
neat / straight *[US]* sans eau ni glace
nectarine brugnon, nectarine
nettle ortie
no smoking défense de fumer
non-smoking area section non fumeurs
noodles nouilles
nut noix
   almond amande
   brazil nut noix du Brésil
   cashew nut noix d'acajou, noix de cajou
   chestnut marron
   cobnut noisette
   coconut noix de coco
   hazelnut noisette, aveline
   peanut arachide, cacah(o)uète
   pecan nut noix de pécan, noix de pacane
   sweet chestnut châtaigne; marron
   walnut noix; cerneau (de la noix)
nutmeg noix de muscade

Oo

oatcake biscuit à la farine d'avoine *[pour manger avec le fromage]*
oatmeal farine d'avoine

oats avoine
   porridge/rolled oats flocons d'avoine
octopus poulpe
oil huile
okra gombo
olive olive
   black olives olives noires
   green olives olives vertes
olive oil huile d'olive
omelette omelette
on the rocks *[with ice]* avec glace, on the rocks
onion oignon
   onion soup soupe à l'oignon
orange orange
   orange juice jus d'orange
   orange sauce sauce à l'orange; *[amère]* sauce bigarade
oregano origan
ostrich autruche
oven four
overdone trop cuit(e)
oxtail queue de boeuf
   oxtail soup soupe à la queue de boeuf
ox tongue langue de boeuf
oyster huître
oyster mushroom pleurote

English-French

Pp

pancake crêpe
pan-fried à la poêle, poêlé(e)
papaya papaye
paprika paprika

par-boiled pré-cuit(e); mi-cuit(e)
parfait parfait
parma ham jambon de Parme
parmesan (cheese) parmesan
parsley persil
   curly parsley persil frisé
   flat parsley persil plat
   parsley sauce sauce au persil *[béchamel fortement persillée]*
parsnip panais
partridge perdrix; *[young]* perdreau
pasta pâtes (alimentaires)
   fresh pasta pâtes fraîches
pastry pâtisserie
   filo pastry pâte (à pâtisserie) très mince
   puff pastry pâte feuilletée
pasty chausson avec viande et pommes de terre
pâté pâté
   liver pâté pâté de foie gras
pawpaw papaye
pea pois
   green peas petits pois
   green pea soup potage St Germain
   split peas pois cassés
   pea soup *[with split peas]* soupe aux pois (cassés)
peach pêche
peanut arachide
   peanut butter beurre de cacahouètes, d'arachides
pear poire
pearl barley orge perlée
pease-pudding purée de pois cassés
pecan nut noix de pécan, noix de pacane
   pecan pie tarte aux noix de pécan
peel *[verb]* peler; éplucher
peel *[noun]* pelure; peau; écorce
   grated peel zeste, écorce râpée
peeled sans pelure; sans peau
pepper *[spice]* poivre
   black, green, white pepper poivre noir, vert, blanc
   ground pepper poivre moulu

   whole pepper   poivre en grains
   pepper mill   moulin à poivre
   pepper pot   poivrière
   pepper steak   steak au poivre
pepper *[vegetable]*   poivron
   green pepper   poivron vert
   red pepper   poivron rouge
   stuffed pepper   poivron farci
peppermint   menthe poivrée
perch   perche (d'eau douce)
perry   cidre de poire
persimmon   plaquemine, kaki
pesto   pistou
petits fours   petits fours
pheasant   faisan
pickled cabbage   choucroute
pickled gherkin/cucumber   cornichon (saumuré, au vinaigre)
pickled herring   hareng mariné
pickled onion   oignon au vinaigre
pickles   pickles
pie   tarte; tourte
pig   porc, cochon
   suck(l)ing pig   cochon de lait, porcelet
pigeon   pigeon
pig's trotters   pieds de porc
pike   brochet
pike-perch   sandre
pilchard   pilchard, (grosse) sardine
pineapple   ananas
pistachio (nut)   pistache
pitcher   pichet, carafe
pitta bread   pain grec *[sans levain]*
plaice   plie, carrelet
plantain   banane verte *[à cuire]*
plat du jour   plat du jour
plate   assiette
plum   prune
plum pudding   plum pudding, pouding de Noël

English-French

plum tomato   tomate oblongue, tomate allongée
poach   pocher
poached   poché(e)
poached egg   oeuf poché
polenta   polenta, semoule de maïs
pollack   lieu
pomegranate   grenade
popcorn   maïs soufflé (sucré, salé)
porcini mushroom   cèpe
pork   porc
   pork chop   côte de porc
   pork crackling   couenne croquante (du rôti de porc)
porridge   porridge, bouillie d'avoine
port   (vin de) porto
pot roast   viande en cocotte
potato   pomme de terre
   baked potato   pomme de terre au four
   fried potoatoes   pommes de terre sautées
   mashed potatoes   purée de pommes de terre, pommes purée
   new potatoes   pommes de terre nouvelles
   potato chips   (pommes) frites
   potato crisps   (pommes) chips
   potato dumpling   gnocchi Parmentier
   potato salad   salade de pommes de terre
potted shrimp   petite terrine de crevettes au beurre
poultry   volaille
pound cake   gâteau quatre-quarts
poussin   poussin
prawn   bouquet, crevette rose; langoustine
preserves   conserves
price   prix
prime rib   côte de boeuf *[première qualité]*
profiteroles   profiteroles
prune   pruneau (sec)
pudding *[savoury]*   pouding
pudding *[sweet]*   dessert; pouding, pudding
pudding rice   riz rond
pudding wine   vin de dessert, vin doux

puff pastry pâte feuilletée
pulses légumineuses
pumpkin potiron, citrouille
purslane pourpier

Qq

English-French

quail caille
   quails eggs oeufs de cailles
quark quark, fromage blanc
quiche quiche
   quiche lorraine quiche lorraine
quince coing
quorn pâté de soja

Rr

rabbit lapin; *[young]* lapereau
rack carré
   rack of lamb carré d'agneau
   rack of ribs carré (d'agneau, de porc)
radicchio trévise, chicorée rouge
radish/radishes radis
ragout ragoût
rainbow trout truite arc-en-ciel
raisin raisin sec

ramekin *[food]*   ramequin
ramekin *[small container]*   ramequin
rancid   rance
rare (steak, meat)   saignant(e)
raspberry   framboise
ravioli   ravioli
raw   cru(e)
recipe   recette
red cabbage   chou rouge
red chilli   piment fort, piment rouge
redcurrant   groseille rouge
   redcurrant jelly   gelée de groseilles
redfish   rascasse
red mullet   rouget barbet
red pepper   poivron rouge, piment doux rouge
red wine   vin rouge
reindeer   chevreuil
rhubarb   rhubarbe
ribs   côtes
   rack of ribs   carré (d'agneau, de porc)
   ribs of beef   côtes de boeuf; entrecôtes
   spare ribs   travers de porc; côtes levées
rice   riz
   rice paper   papier de riz
   rice pudding   pouding au riz; riz au lait *[cuit au four]*
   risotto rice   riz pour risotto *[riz rond du Piémont]*
   wild rice   riz sauvage
ripe   mûr(e)
rissole   rissole
river   rivière; *[poisson]* d'eau douce
roast *[verb]*   rôtir
   roast beef   rôti de boeuf, rosbif
   roast chicken   poulet rôti
   roast pork   rôti de porc
roasted   rôti(e)
rock salt   sel gemme
rocket   roquette
rockfish   rascasse

roe   oeufs de poisson
   hard roe   oeufs de poisson
   soft roe   laitance
roll *[bread]*   petit pain
rolled oats   flocons d'avoine
rollmop herring   rollmop, hareng roulé (mariné)
romaine (lettuce)   romaine
room temperature   chambré(e)
rosé (wine)   (vin) rosé
rosehip   fruit de l'églantier
rosemary   romarin
rum   rhum
   rum baba   baba au rhum
rump steak   romsteak
runner bean   haricot grimpant
rusk   biscotte *[pour bébé]*
rye   seigle
rye bread   pain de seigle; pumpernickel
rye whisky   rye *[whisky de seigle]*

Ss

saccharin   saccharine
saddle   râble (de lapin); selle (d'agneau)
safflower   carthame
saffron   safran
sage   sauge
sago   sagou
saithe   lieu noir
salad   salade
   green salad   salade verte
   mixed salad   salade composée, salade panachée

salad dressing vinaigrette; mayonnaise; sauce
salad cream crème mayonnaise
side salad salade verte *[en accompagnement]*
salami saucisson italien
salmon saumon
salmon steak darne de saumon
salmon trout truite de mer; truite saumonée
salsify salsifis
salt sel
low-salt hyposodé(e)
salted salé(e); avec sel
sand sole sole *[plus petite que la 'vraie sole']*
sandwich sandwich
sardine sardine
sauce sauce
white sauce (sauce) bechamel, sauce blanche
saucer soucoupe
saury balaou
sausage saucisse
liver sausage leberwurst
sausage roll friand
sautéed sauté(e)
saveloy cervelas
savoury entremets salé
savoy cabbage chou vert frisé *[pommé]*
saxifrage saxifrage
scallion *[US]* ciboule, cive
scallop coquille St Jacques
scalloped chicken *[US]* poulet en sauce blanche, au four
scalloped potatoes *[US]* gratin dauphinois
scampi queues de langoustine, scampi
scone *[UK]* scone *[petit pain qu'on mange avec confiture et crème]*
scotch à l'écossaise
scotch broth potage de mouton, légumes et orge
scotch egg oeuf en croquette *[oeuf (dur) enrobé de chair à saucisse, pané et frit]*
scrambled eggs oeufs brouillés
sea bass, bass loup (de mer), bar

sea bream　brème de mer
seafood　fruits de mer
sear　(faire) saisir
seasoning　assaisonnement
sea trout　truite de mer
seaweed　algue
semolina　semoule
service　service
　　discretionary　à la discrétion du client
　　included　compris
　　not included　non compris
serviette　serviette (de table)
sesame seeds　graines de sésame
shad　alose
shallot　échalote
shark　requin; aiguillat
sharp　fort(e); acide
shellfish　crustacé, coquillage; fruits de mer
shepherd's pie　hachis Parmentier
sherbet　sorbet; granité
sherry　xérès
shiitake mushrooms　champignons chinois (shiitake)
shortbread　sablé
shortcrust (pastry)　pâte brisée
shoulder　épaule; palette
shrimp　crevette (grise)
　　shrimp cocktail　crevettes mayonnaise
sift　tamiser
silverside　gîte à la noix
simmer　(laisser) mijoter
single cream　crème (légère)
sippets　pain qu'on trempe dans un liquide
sirloin　aloyau; faux-filet
skate　raie
skewer　brochette
skimmed milk　lait écrémé
skin　peau; pelure
skipjack　bonite

slice tranche
   slice of bread tranche de pain
   slice of pie part de tarte
   slice of ham tranche de jambon
sliced tranché(e)
sloe prunelle
   sloe gin eau de vie de prunelle
smelt éperlan
smoked fumé(e)
   smoked bacon lard fumé
   smoked cheese fromage fumé
   smoked eel anguille fumée
   smoked fish poisson fumé
   smoked haddock aiglefin fumé
   smoked kipper hareng saur, hareng fumé
   smoked meat viande fumé
   smoked salmon saumon fumé
snail escargot
snipe bécassine
soda bread pain au bicarbonate de soude
soda water eau de seltz
soft-boiled egg oeuf à la coque
soft cheese fromage à pâte molle
soft drink boisson (gazeuse) non alcoolisée
soft roe laitance
sole sole
sorbet sorbet
sorghum sorgho
sorrel oseille
soufflé soufflé
   cheese soufflé soufflé au fromage
soup soupe; potage
   soup spoon cuillère à soupe
   beef tea bouillon de boeuf
   broth bouillon
   chowder soupe de poisson et légumes à base de lait
   fish broth court-bouillon
   fish soup soupe de poisson(s)
   mulligatawny potage au cari

onion soup   soupe à l'oignon
vegetable soup   soupe de légumes; minestrone
vichyssoise   vichyssoise
sour   aigre
sour cream   crème aigre
sweet and sour   aigre-doux (-douce)
soy bean, soya bean, soja bean   (fève de) soja
soy sauce, soya sauce   sauce soja
spaghetti   spaghetti
spare ribs   travers de porc; côtes levées
sparkling   pétillant(e)
   water   eau gazeuse
   wine   vin mousseux; vin pétillant
spice   épice
spicy   épicé(e)
spinach   épinard
spiny lobster   langouste
sponge biscuits   biscuits à la cuillère
sponge cake   gâteau mousseline; génoise
spoon   cuillère, cuiller
sprat   sprat, harenguet, anchois de Norvège
spring greens   jeunes feuilles de choux, brocolis, etc.
spring onion   ciboule, cive
spring water   eau de source
sprouts (Brussels)   choux de Bruxelles
squab   pigeonneau
squash   courge
squid   calmar, encornet
stale   rassis(e)
starter   entrée
steak (beef)   bifteck, steak
steak and kidney pie   pie de bifteck et rognons
steak and kidney pudding   pouding de bifteck et rognons
steamed   (cuit) à la vapeur
stew *[meat]*   fricassée, ragoût
   lamb stew   navarin
stewed   *[meat]* (en) fricassée; *[fruit]* en compote
   stewed fruit   compote de fruits, fruits en compote

English-French

stewed steak fricassée, ragoût de boeuf

stilton fromage stilton

stir-fry sauter à la chinoise

stout stout *[bière brune]*

straight *[US]* / **neat** sans eau ni glace

strawberry fraise
   strawberry jam confiture de fraises
   strawberry shortcake gâteau fourré aux fraises, recouvert de crème Chantilly

streaky bacon lard de poitrine, poitrine fumée

strip steak entrecôte

stuffed farci(e); fourré(e)
   stuffed olives olives farcies

stuffing farce

sturgeon esturgeon

suck(l)ing pig cochon de lait, porcelet

suet suif (de boeuf)

sugar sucre
   caster sugar sucre semoule
   granulated sugar sucre granulé
   icing sugar sucre en poudre; sucre glace

sugar snap peas petit pois gourmands; pois mange-tout

sultanas raisins de Smyrne

sundae coupe glacée

sunflower tournesol
   sunflower oil huile de tournesol

supper dîner; souper

swede navet (de Suède), chou-navet

sweet sucré(e); doux (douce)
   sweet (wine) (vin) doux; vin de dessert
   sweet chesnut châtaigne, marron
   sweet potato patate douce
   sweet trolley desserts *[présentés sur une table roulante]*

sweet and sour aigre-doux (-douce)

sweetbreads ris de veau

sweetcorn maïs (en épis, en grains)

swiss roll (gâteau) roulé

swordfish espadon

syllabub   syllabub; sabayon
syrup   sirop

Tt

table   table
   tablecloth   nappe
   tablespoon   cuillère à dessert
   table wine   vin de table
tagliatelle   tagliatelle
tangerine   tangerine
tapioca   tapioca
taragon, tarragon   estragon
tart   tartelette
tartar sauce   sauce tartare
tea   thé
   afternoon tea   (le) thé de 5 heures
   beef tea   bouillon de boeuf
   cup of tea   tasse de thé
   herbal tea   tisane, infusion
   high-tea   repas de 5 heures *[Ecosse et Nord de l'Angleterre]*
   iced tea   thé glacé
   lemon tea   thé (au) citron
   teacake   brioche *[coupée, grillée, avec beurre, servie avec du thé]*
   tea spoon   cuillère à thé
   tea with milk   thé au lait
   tea-time   heure du thé
   teapot   théière
tench   tanche
tender   tendre
tenderloin   filet (de boeuf, de porc)
terrine   terrine
thrush   grive

thyme thym
tin boîte de conserve
tinned en boîte (de conserve)
tip pourboire
toad in the hole saucisses couvertes de pâte *[au four]*
toast pain grillé; rôtie
   french toast pain perdu, pain doré
toffee caramel (au beurre)
tofu tofu, pâté de soja
tomato tomate
   tomato juice jus de tomate
   tomato ketchup ketchup, sauce tomate
   tomato salad salade de tomate
   tomato sauce sauce (à la) tomate
tongue langue *[de boeuf]*
toothpick cure-dent(s)
tope milandre
treacle mélasse
   treacle tart tarte au sirop de maïs
trifle trifle *[génoise, fruits, Chantilly]*
trimmings accompagnement, garniture
tripe tripes; gras-double
trout truite
truffle truffe
   chocolate truffle (sweet) truffe (au chocolat)
   truffle butter beurre de truffes
tuna, tunny thon
turbot turbot
turkey dinde
   roast turkey dinde rôtie
turmeric curcuma
turnip navet
turnip tops fanes de navet
turnover chausson (aux pommes, etc.)

Uu

uncooked cru(e); qui n'est pas cuit(e)
underdone pas assez cuit(e)
unsalted butter beurre sans sel
upside-down cake gâteau renversé

Vv

vanilla vanille
   vanilla essence extrait de vanille *[liquide]*
   vanilla ice cream glace à la vanille
   vanilla pod/bean gousse de vanille
   vanilla sugar sucre vanillé
veal veau
   veal escalope escalope de veau
vegetable légume
   vegetable soup soupe de légumes; minestrone
vegetarian végétarien (-ienne)
venison venaison; chevreuil; gibier *[à poil]*
vermicelli vermicelle
very dry (wine) très sec
victoria sponge (cake) génoise
vinaigrette vinaigrette
vinegar vinaigre
vine leaves feuilles de vigne
virgin olive oil huile d'olive vierge
vol au vent vol-au-vent, bouchée feuilletée; timbale
   chicken vol au vent bouchée à la reine

Ww

wafer   gaufrette

waffles   gaufres

waiter   garçon, serveur

waitress   serveuse

Waldorf salad   salade Waldorf (pommes, céleri, noix, avec mayonnaise)

walnut   noix; cerneau (de la noix)

water   eau

  bottled water   eau en bouteille

  glass of water   verre d'eau

  iced water   eau glacée, très froide

  jug of water   carafe d'eau

  sparkling water/fizzy water   eau gazeuse

  spring/mineral water   eau de source; eau minérale

  still water   eau plate, non gazeuse

watercress   cresson de fontaine

water melon   pastèque

well done   bien cuit(e)

welsh rarebit, rabbit   pain avec fromage grillé

whale   baleine

wheat   blé

whelk   buccin

whipped cream   crème Chantilly, crème fouettée

whisky   whisky écossais

whitebait *[sprats]*   blanchaille

white (wine, meat)   (vin) blanc; (viande) blanche

white bread   pain de mie; pain blanc

white wine   vin blanc

whiting   merlan

whole grain mustard   moutarde de Meaux

wholemeal bread   pain complet

whortleberry   myrtille

wild rice riz sauvage
wild strawberry fraise des bois, fraise sauvage
wine vin
   bottle of wine bouteille de vin
   wine cooler rafraîchisseur *[à vin]*
   glass of wine verre de vin
   house wine vin (de la) maison
   local wine vin local; vin de pays
   red wine vin rouge
   sparkling wine vin mousseux; vin pétillant
   sweet/pudding wine vin doux, vin de dessert
   wine list carte des vins
   wine vinegar vinaigre de vin (rouge, blanc)
   wine waiter sommelier
   white wine vin blanc
winkle bigorneau
woodcock bécasse

English-French

Yy

yam igname; *[US]* patate douce
yoghurt yaourt, yogourt
   plain yoghurt yaourt nature
yorkshire pudding yorkshire pudding *[beignet de pâte frite, salé]*

Zz

zabaglione zabaglione
zest zeste
zucchini *[US]* courgette

Wines and spirits

by John Doxat

Major French wine regions

Alsace

Producer of attractive, light white wines, mostly medium-dry, widely used as carafe wines in middle-range French restaurants. Alsace wines are not greatly appreciated overseas and thus remain comparatively inexpensive for their quality; they are well placed to compete with popular German varieties. Alsace wines are designated by grape - principally Sylvaner for lightest styles, the widespread and reliable Riesling for a large part of the total, and Gerwürtztraminer for slightly fruitier wines.

Bordeaux

Divided into a score of districts, and sub-divided into very many *communes* (parishes). The big district names are Médoc, St Emilion, Pomerol, Graves and Sauternes. Prices for the great reds (châteaux Pétrus, Mouton-Rothschild, etc.) or the finest sweet whites (especially the miraculous Yquem) have become stratospheric. Yet 'château' in itself means little and the classification of various rankings of châteaux is not easily understood. Some tiny vineyards are entitled to be called château, which has led to disputes about what have been dubbed 'phantom châteaux'. Visitors are advised, unless wine-wise, to stick to the simpler designations.

Bourgogne (Burgundy)

Topographically a large region, stretching from Chablis (on the east end of the Loire), noted for its steely dry whites, to Lyons. It is particularly associated with fairly powerful red wines and very dry whites, which tend to acidity except for the costlier styles. Almost to Bordeaux excesses, the prices for really top Burgundies have gone through the roof. For value, stick to simpler local wines.

Technically Burgundies, but often separately listed, are the Beaujolais wines. The young red Beaujolais (not necessarily the over-publicised *nouveau*) are delicious when mildly chilled. There are several rather neglected Beaujolais wines (Moulin-à-Vent, Morgon, St Amour, for instance) that improve for several years: they represent good value as a rule. The Maçonnais and Chalonnais also produce sound Burgundies (red and white) that are usually priced within reason.

Wine

Champagne

So important is Champagne that, alone of French wines, it carries no AC (*appellation contrôlée*): its name is sufficient guarantee. (It shares this distinction with the brandies Cognac and Armagnac.) Vintage Champagnes from the grandes marques - a limited number of 'great brands' - tend to be as expensive in France as in Britain. You can find unknown brands of high quality (often off-shoots of grandes marques) at attractive prices, especially in the Champagne country itself. However, you need information to discover these, and there are true Champagnes for the home market that are doux (sweet) or demi-sec (medium sweet) that are pleasing to few non-French tastes. Champagne is very closely controlled as to region, quantities, grape types, and is made only by secondary fermentation in the bottle. From 1993, it is prohibited (under EU law) to state that other wines are made by the 'champagne method' - even if they are.

Loire

Prolific producer of very reliable, if rarely great, white wines, notably Muscadet, Sancerre, Anjou (its *rosé* is famous), Vouvray (sparkling and semi-sparkling), and Saumur (particularly its 'champagne styles'). Touraine makes excellent whites and also reds of some distinction - Bourgueil and Chinon. It used to be widely believed - a rumour put out by rivals? - that Loire wines 'did not travel': nonsense. They are a successful export.

Rhône

Continuation south of Burgundy. The Rhône is particularly associated with very robust reds, notably Châteauneuf-du-Pape, and also with Tavel, arguably the finest of all still rosé wines. Lirac rosé is nearly as good. Hermitage and Gigondas are names to respect for reds, whites and rosés. Rhône has well earned its modern reputation - no longer Burgundy's poorer brother. From the extreme south comes the newly 'smart' dessert *vin doux naturel,* ultrasweet *Muscat des Beaumes-de-Venise,* once despised by British wine-drinkers. There are fashions in wine just like anything else.

Wine

Minor regions

Bergerac   Attractive basic reds; also sweet Monbazillac, relished in France but not easily obtained outside: aged examples can be superb.

Cahors   Noted for its powerful *vin de pays* 'black wine', darkest red made.

Corsica   Roughish wines of more antiquity than breeding, but by all means drink local reds - and try the wine-based aperitif Cap Corse - if visiting this remarkable island.

Gaillac   Little known; once celebrated for dessert wines.

Jura   Virtually unknown outside France. Try local speciality wines such as *vin jaune* if in the region.

Jurançon   Remote area; sound, unimportant white wines, sweet styles being the better.

Midi   Stretches from Marseilles to the Spanish border. Outstandingly prolific contributor to the 'EU wine lake' and producer of some 80 per cent of French *vins de table*, white and red. Sweet whites dominate, and there is major production of *vins doux naturels* (fortified sugary wines).

Paris   Yes, there is a vineyard - in Montmartre! Don't ask for a bottle: the tiny production is sold by auction, for charity, to rich collectors of curiosities.

Provence   Large wine region of immense antiquity. Many and varied *vins de pays* of little distinction. Best known for rosé, usually on the sweet side; all inexpensive and totally drinkable.

Savoy   Good enough table wines for local consumption. Best product of the region is delicious Chambéry vermouth: as an aperitif, do try the well distributed Chambéryzette, a unique vermouth with a hint of wild strawberries.

Wine

Spirits

The great French spirit is brandy. Cognac, commercially the leader, must come from the closely controlled region of that name. Of various quality designations, the commonest is VSOP (very special old pale): it will be a cognac worth drinking neat. Remember, *champagne* in a cognac connotation has absolutely no connection with the wine. It is a topographical term, with *grande champagne* being the most prestigious cognac area; fine champagne is a blend of brandy from the two top cognac sub-divisions. Armagnac has become better known lately outside

France, and rightly so. As a brandy it has a much longer history than cognac: some connoisseurs rate old armagnac (the quality designations are roughly similar) above cognac.

Be cautious of French brandy without a cognac or armagnac title, regardless of how many meaningless 'stars' the label carries or even the magic word 'Napoleon' (which has no legal significance).

Little appreciated in Britain is the splendid 'apple brandy', Calvados, mainly associated with Normandy but also made in Brittany and the Marne. The best is *Calvados du Pays d'Auge*. Do taste well-aged Calvados, but avoid any suspiciously cheap.

Contrary to popular belief, true Calvados is not distilled from cider - but an inferior imitation is: French cider (cidre) is excellent.

Though most French proprietary aperitifs, like Dubonnet, are fairly low in alcohol, the extremely popular Pernod/Ricard pastis-style brands are highly spirituous. Eau-de-vie is the generic term for all spirits, but colloquially tends to refer to local, often rough, distillates. Exceptions are the better *alcools blancs* (white spirits), which are not inexpensive, made from fresh fruits and not sweetened as *crèmes* are.

Wine

Glossary of French wine terms

Abricotine   Generic apricot liqueur: look for known brands.

Alcool blanc   Spirit distilled from various fruits (not wine); not fruit-flavoured cordials.

Aligoté   Light dry Burgundy.

Alsace   *See* Outline of wine regions, p102

Anis   Aniseed, much favoured in pastis (Ricard/Pernod) type aperitifs.

Anjou   *See* Loire, Outline of wine regions, p103

Aperitif   Literally 'opener': any drink taken as an appetiser.

Appellation (d'origine) Contrôllée   or AC wine, whose label will give you a good deal of information, will usually be costlier - but not necessarily better - than one that is a VDQS 'designated (regional) wine of superior quality'. A newer, marginally lesser category is VQPRD: 'quality wine from a specified district'. Hundreds of wines bear AC descriptions: you require knowledge and/or a wine guide to find your way around. The intention of the AC laws was to protect consumers and ensure wine was not falsely labelled - and also to prevent over-production. Only wines of reasonable standards should achieve AC status: new ones (some rather suspect) are being regularly admitted to the list.

Armagnac   *See* Sprits, p104

Barsac   Very sweet Sauternes of varying quality.

Basserau   A bit of an oddity: sparkling red Burgundy.

Beaumes-de-Venise   Well-known vin doux naturel; see Provence, Minor Regions.

Beaune   Famed red Burgundy; costly.

Bergerac   Sound red wine from south-west France.

Blanc de Blancs   White wine from white grapes alone. Sometimes confers extra quality but by no means always. White wine made from black grapes (the skins removed before fermentation) is Blanc de Noirs. Carries no special quality connotation in itself.

Bordeaux   *See* Outline of wine regions, p102

Bourgeuil   Reliable red Loire wine.

Bourgogne   Burgundy; see Outline of wine regions.

Brut   Very dry; description particularly applicable to best sparkling wines.

Brut Sauvage   Dry to the point of displeasing acidness to most palates; very rare though a few good wines carry the description.

Cabernet   Noble grape, especially Cabernet-Sauvignon for excellent, if not absolutely top grade, red wines.

Wine

Cacao   Cocoa; basis of a popular crème.

Calvados   *See* Hints on spirits, p104

Cassis   Blackcurrant; notably in crème de cassis (see Kir).

Cave   Cellar.

Cépage   Indicates grape variety; e.g. Cépage Cabernet-Sauvignon.

Chablis   *See* Burgundy, Outline of wine regions, p102.

Chai   Ground-level storehouse, wholly employed in Cognac and sometimes in Bordeaux and other districts.

Champagne   *See* Outline of wine regions, p103. Also specialty note Méthode Traditionnelle below.

Château(x)   *See* Outline of wine regions, Bordeaux, p102

Châteauneuf-du-Pape   Best known of powerful Rhône red wines.

Chenin-blanc   Grape variety associated with many fine Loire wines.

Clairet   Unimportant Bordeaux wine, its distinction being probable origin of English word Claret.

Clos   Mainly a Burgundian term for a vineyard formerly (rarely now) enclosed by a wall.

Cognac   *See* Hints on spirits, p104

Corbières   Usually a sound south of France red wine.

Côte   Indicates vineyard on a hillside; no quality connotation necessarily.

Côteau(x)   Much the same as above.

Crème   Many sweet, sometimes sickly, mildly alcoholic cordials with many local specialities. Nearer to true liqueurs are top makes of crème de menthe and crème de Grand Marnier (q.v.). Crème de cassis is mixed with white wine to produce kir or with a sparkling white wine to produce kir royale.

Crémant   Sparkling wine with strong but rather brief effervescence.

Cru   Literally 'growth'; somewhat complicated and occasionally misleading term: e.g. grand cru may be only grower's estimation, cru classé just means the wine is officially recognised, but grand cru classé is most likely to be something special.

Cuve close   Literally 'sealed vat'. Describes production of sparkling wines by bulk as opposed to individual bottle fermentation. Can produce satisfactory wines and certainly much superior to cheap carbonated styles.

Cuvée   Should mean unblended wine from single vat, but cuvée spéciale may not be particularly special: only taste will tell.

Wine

Demi-sec   Linguistically misleading, as it does not mean 'half-dry' but 'medium sweet'.

Domaine   Broadly, Burgundian equivalent to Bordeaux château.

Doux   Very sweet.

Eau-de-vie   Generic term for all distilled spirits but usually only applied in practice to roughish marc (q.v.) and the like.

Entre-deux-Mers   Undistinguished but fairly popular white Bordeaux.

Frappé   Drink served with crushed ice; viz. crème de menthe frappée.

Fleurie   One of several superior Beaujolais wines.

Glacé   Drink chilled by immersion of bottle in ice or in refrigerator, as distinct from frappé above.

Goût   Taste; also colloquial term in some regions for local eau-de-vie (q.v.).

Grand Marnier   Distinguished orange-flavoured liqueur. See also crème.

Haut   'High'. It indicates upper part of wine district, not necessarily the best, though Haut-Médoc produces much better wines than other areas.

Hermitage   Several excellent Rhône red wines carry this title.

Izarra   Ancient Armagnac-based liqueur much favoured by its Basque originators.

Juliénas   Notable Beaujolais wine.

Kir   Well-chilled dry white wine (should be Bourgogne Aligoté) plus a teaspoon of crème de cassis (q.v.). Made with champagne (or good dry sparkling wine) it is Kir Royal.

Liqueur   From old liqueur de dessert, denoting postprandial digestive. Always very sweet. 'Liqueur' has become misused as indication of superior quality: to speak of 'liqueur cognac' is contradictory - yet some very fine true liqueurs are based on cognac.

Loire   *See* Outline of wine regions, p103

Marc   Mostly coarse distillations from wine residue with strong local popularity. A few marcs ('mar') - de Champagne, de Bourgogne especially - have achieved a certain cult status.

Marque   Brand or company name.

Méthode Traditionnelle   Since the labelling ban prohibiting the use of the term 'champagne method' for wines made outside the Champagne district, this term is used for superior sparkling wine made in the same way as champagne, by fermentation in bottle

Meursault   Splendid white Burgundy for those who can afford it.

Wine

Minervoise   Respectable southern red wine: can be good value as are many such.

Mise   As in mise en bouteilles au château ('château-bottled'), or ... dans nos caves ('in our cellars') and variations.

Montrachet   Very fine white Burgundy.

Moulin-à-Vent   One of the rather special Beaujolais wines.

Muscadet   Arguably the most popular light dry Loire white wine.

Muscat   Though used for some dry whites, this grape is mainly associated with succulent dessert-style wines.

Nouveau   New wine, for drinking fresh; particularly associated with now tiring vogue for Beaujolais Nouveau.

Pastis   General term for powerful anis/liquorice aperitifs originally evolved to replace banned absinthe and particularly associated with Marseilles area through the great firm of Ricard.

Pétillant   Gently, naturally effervescent.

Pineau   Unfermented grape juice lightly fortified with grape spirit; attractive aperitif widely made in France and under-appreciated abroad.

Pouilly-Fuissé   Dry white Burgundy (Macon); sometimes over-valued.

Pouilly-Fumé   Easily confused with above; a very dry fine Loire white.

Porto   Port wine: usually lighter in France than the type preferred in Britain and popular, chilled, as an aperitif.

Primeur   More or less the same as nouveau, but more often used for fine vintage wine sold en primeur for laying down to mature.

Rosé   'Pink wine', best made by allowing temporary contact of juice and black grapes during fermentation; also by mixing red and white wine.

Sauvignon   Notable white grape; see also Cabernet.

Sec   'Dry', but a wine so marked will be sweetish, even very sweet. Extra Sec may actually mean on the dry side.

Sirop   Syrup; e.g. sugar-syrup used in mixed drinks, also some flavoured proprietary non-alcoholic cordials.

Supérieur(e)   Much the same as Haut (q.v.) except in VDQS.

VQRPD   *See* Appellation (d'origine) Contrôllée above, p107

Vin de Xeres   Sherry ('vin de 'ereth').

Wine

Classic French Sauces

abricot, sauce   Apricot sauce

airelles, sauce   Cranberry sauce

Albert, sauce   Horseradish simmered in white bouillon, cream and breadcrumbs added, together with English mustard, vinegar and parsley

albufera, sauce   Sauce suprême mixed with meat glaze and pimento butter

allemande, sauce   White velouté sauce thickened with egg yolks. [also called *sauce parisienne*]

américaine, sauce   The cooking liquor from lobster mixed with the lobster coral and cream, finished with parsley

anchois, sauce   Anchovy sauce

andalouse, sauce   Mayonnaise mixed with tomato purée and garnished with julienned red sweet pepper

anglaise, sauce   *see*   **crème à l'anglaise**

anglaise, sauce à l'   *see*   **egg custard sauce**

aurore maigre, sauce   As *sauce aurore* but using fish stock. Used for fish

aurore, sauce   Suprême sauce, lightly flavoured with tomato purée. Used for boiled chicken, poached eggs, etc.

bâtarde, sauce   Water and white roux with egg yolks, cream and a little lemon juice. Served with asparagus or poached fish. [also called *sauce au beurre*]

bavaroise, sauce   *Hollandaise* sauce flavoured with grated horseradish

béarnaise tomatée, sauce   *see*   **sauce choron**

béarnaise, sauce   As *Hollandaise* sauce but thicker and with tarragon. Served warm with grilled meat and fish

béchamel, sauce   A basic white sauce made from a white roux and seasoned milk. A very important base and often referred to simply as béchamel

Bercy, sauce   Chopped shallots cooked in butter with white wine and fish stock added.

beurre, sauce au   *see*   **sauce bâtarde**

bigarade, sauce   Sauce made from the residues of duck with Seville orange and lemon juice. [also called *orange sauce*]

bolognaise, sauce   *see*   **Bolognese sauce**

bonnefoy, sauce   A white bordelaise sauce made with dry white instead of red wine and a white velouté instead of espagnole sauce. [also called *sauce bordelaise au vin blanc*]

bordelaise au vin blanc, sauce *see* **sauce bonnefoy**

bordelaise, sauce A brown sauce made from red wine, shallots, thyme, bay leaf and pepper.

bourguignonne, sauce Red wine flavoured with chopped shallots or onions, mushrooms, parsley, thyme and bay leaf. Served with grilled or roast beef. [also called *Burgundy sauce*]

bretonne, sauce (For haricot beans) onions fried in butter, with white wine, Espagnole sauce, a little tomato sauce and garlic added. (For fish) fish velouté mixed with finely-chopped leek, celery, onion and mushrooms.

canotière, sauce Cooking liquor from poached freshwater fish reduced by two thirds, thickened with beurre manié, simmered 5 minutes, strained and finished with butter and a little cayenne pepper

câpres, sauce aux Butter sauce with capers added. Served with boiled fish

cardinal, sauce A pink sauce based on lobster and truffles, served with fish

cerises, sauce aux *see* **cherry sauce**

champignons, sauce aux 1) For meat see *mushroom sauce*. 2) For fish: fish velouté, with sliced mushrooms. Served with boiled or poached fish

chantilly, sauce A thick mayonnaise with stiffly whipped cream added at the last moment. [also called *mayonnaise chantilly*]

charcutière, sauce As for *Robert sauce* but finished with a julienne of gherkins

chateaubriand, sauce White wine with shallots, thyme, bayleaf and mushroom trimmings, brown veal stock, and finished with chopped tarragon. Used with red meat

chevreuil, sauce As *sauce poivrade* but with bacon or game added. Finished with a little sugar and cayenne pepper. Served with game.

Chivry, sauce White wine boiled with chervil, parsley, tarragon, and chopped shallots, mixed with velouté sauce and finished with beurre à la Chivry. Served with boiled and poached chicken

choron, sauce A *béarnaise sauce* with tomato purée. [also called *sauce béarnaise tomatée*]

crevettes, sauce aux Boiling fish velouté finished with shrimps

currie à l'indienne, sauce Finely sliced onion cooked in butter with mace, a cinnamon stick, and curry powder, then mixed with coconut milk and veal or fish stock. [also called *sauce indienne*]

currie, sauce Curry sauce made with white bouillon

Sauces

demi-glace, sauce A mixture of equal parts of *espagnole sauce* and brown stock reduced. Used as a basis for other sauces

diable, sauce A reduction of chopped shallots, white wine, vinegar, cayenne pepper and mignonette pepper. Served with fried or grilled fish or meat. [also called *devilled sauce*]

diane, sauce A *poivrade* sauce enriched with cream

diplomate, sauce *Sauce normande* with lobster butter, garnished with truffles and diced lobster meat. Served with whole large fish

doria, sauce *Béchamel sauce* with cream, chopped cucumber and grated nutmeg. Served with fish

duchesse, sauce Tomato and Hollandaise sauces combined with chopped ham and white wine

duxelles, sauce White wine and mushroom cooking liquor with shallots mixed with demi-glace sauce, tomato purée and duxelles. Used for gratinated dishes

épicurienne, sauce Mayonnaise flavoured with gherkins and smooth chutney. Served with cold meat, eggs, poultry and fish

espagnole, sauce (Brown sauce) one of the three classic basic sauces made from a brown roux mixed with tomato purée and brown stock flavoured with browned vegetables. [also called *brown sauce, Spanish sauce*]

estragon, sauce A velouté sauce based on fish stock with tarragon. Served with fish

financière, sauce Madeira sauce that has been reduced. Served with dishes garnished à la financière

fines herbes, sauce aux White wine boiled with herbs, mixed with demi-glace sauce if required brown or with white velouté sauce if white and finished with herbs and lemon juice

foyot, sauce *Béarnaise sauce* with meat glaze added. [also called *sauce valois*]

genevoise, sauce A mix of vegetables browned in butter with parsley, thyme and bayleaf, cooked with a chopped salmon head and red wine; *espagnole sauce* added and finished with anchovy essence. Served with salmon and trout

génoise, sauce A purée of pistachios, pinenuts and *Béchamel sauce*, mixed with egg yolk, lemon juice and oil

godard, sauce White wine reduced with vegetables, ham, and demi-glace sauce

grand-veneur, sauce A *poivrade sauce* made using game stock. Served with game

gratin, sauce   White wine, fish stock, shallots finished with chopped parsley.

gribiche, sauce   Mashed hard boiled egg yolks blended with oil and vinegar, flavoured with capers and gherkins, tarragon, chervil and parsley. Served with fish

groseilles, sauce   *see*   **gooseberry sauce**

hachée, sauce   Vinegar with fish stock, onion and shallot, thickened with beurre manié, and finished with herbs, capers and duxelles

hollandaise, sauce   Thick sauce made from egg yolks, a little pepper and vinegar, whisked over a gentle heat. Served warm with hot fish and some vegetables

homard, sauce   A lobster-flavoured sauce with tomato purée and fish stock

hongroise, sauce   A velouté sauce flavoured with onion and paprika. [also called *Hungarian sauce*]

huîtres, sauce aux   *Sauce normande* with oysters added. Used for poached fish

hussarde, sauce   White wine, onion, tomato purée, stock and ham; finished with horseradish and parsley. Served with grilled or spit roasted meat

indienne, sauce   *see*   **sauce currie à l'indienne**

italienne, sauce   1) Sauce with ham, tomato, parsley, chervil and tarragon. 2) A cold sauce of poached brain mixed with mayonnaise. Served with cold meats

ivoire, sauce   Suprême sauce with meat glaze added. Used with boiled chicken. [also called *ivory sauce*]

laguipierre, sauce   Butter sauce with lemon and fish glaze. Used for boiled fish

livonienne, sauce   A mix of vegetables and fish velouté, finished with truffle and parsley. Served with fish

lyonnaise, sauce   Onion, vinegar, brown stock. [also called *brown onion sauce*]

madère, sauce   *see*   **Madeira sauce**

maltaise, sauce   *Hollandaise sauce* with orange juice and orange zest. [also called *Maltese sauce*]

marchand de vin, sauce   A *chasseur sauce* based on red wine and stock

marinière, sauce   *Sauce Bercy* with mussel cooking liquor and egg yolks

Sauces

matelote blanche, sauce *Sauce canotière* with small onions and button mushrooms

mayonnaise chantilly *see* **chantilly, sauce**

mayonnaise, sauce Egg yolks, vinegar, French mustard combined, oil poured in slowly with vigorous whisking until thickened. Served cold and used as a base for many other cold sauces

moelle, sauce *Bordelaise sauce* with bone marrow and parsley

Mornay, sauce *see* **cheese sauce**

moscovite, sauce *Poivrade sauce* made with venison stock, sweet wine, juniper berries, currants and pinenuts or almonds

mousquetaire, sauce Mayonnaise flavoured with onion cooked in white wine. Served cold

mousseline, sauce *Hollandaise sauce* mixed with whipped double cream. Sometimes called sauce chantilly

mousseuse, sauce Butter mixed with lemon juice, salt and cream which is then chilled and sliced and served with boiled fish

moutarde, sauce *see* **mustard sauce**

Nantua, sauce *Béchamel sauce* with cream and crayfish butter

Newburg, sauce Lobster cooked with Madeira, cayenne pepper, cream and fish stock, thickened with egg yolks

niçoise, sauce Vinaigrette with French mustard, anchovies, capers, olives and parsley. Served with meat salads and hard boiled eggs

noisette, sauce *Hollandaise sauce* finished with beurre de noisette. Used with poached salmon and trout

normande, sauce A fish velouté sauce with cream, egg yolks and butter. Served with fish and shellfish. [also called *Normandy sauce*]

oeufs, sauce aux *see* **egg sauce**

oignons, sauce aux *see* **onion sauce**

orientale, sauce *Sauce américaine* with curry powder and cream

paloise, sauce *Hollandaise sauce* with mint

parisienne, sauce *see* **sauce allemande**

périgourdine, sauce *Sauce Périgueux* with thick slices of truffle

Périgueux, sauce An *espagnole sauce* with port and finely chopped truffle. Served with meat and omelettes

persil, sauce *see* **parsley sauce**

persillade, sauce Vinaigrette dressing with persillade

piquante, sauce *see* **piquant sauce**

Sauces

poivrade, sauce A mix of vegetables cooked with wine, vinegar, pepper, and demi-glace. Served with venison. [also called *pepper sauce*]

porto, sauce *see* **port-wine sauce**

portugaise, sauce *Espagnole sauce* made with fresh tomatoes instead of tomato purée

poulette, sauce Sauce made from white stock with lemon juice, butter and parsley thickened with egg yolks

provençale, sauce Tomatoes cooked slowly with garlic, parsley, seasoning and a little sugar

raifort, sauce *see* **horseradish sauce**

ravigote, sauce 1) White wine and vinegar mixed with a velouté sauce; finished with chervil, tarragon and chives. Served hot. 2) A vinaigrette made with oil and vinegar, capers, parsley, tarragon, chervil, chives, and onion

Réforme, sauce A mix of vegetables, with vinegar, peppercorns, demi-glace, and red currant jelly added; garnished with beetroot, hard boiled egg white, gherkin, mushroom, truffle and tongue. Served with lamb cutlets

régence, sauce For meat, a mix of vegetables, white wine, demi-glace sauce and truffle essence. For fish and poultry, *sauce normande* with white wine, mushroom and truffle trimmings

relevée, sauce Ketchup

remoulade, sauce *Tartare sauce* with anchovy essence. Served with fried fish

riche, sauce *Sauce diplomate* finished with truffles

Robert, sauce Onion with stock, mustard, and castor sugar added. Served with fried pork chop

romaine, sauce Caramel dissolved in vinegar, *espagnole sauce* and game stock added. Finished with pine nuts and raisins

rouennaise, sauce Hot *bordelaise sauce* mixed with duck liver

Rubens, sauce Fish stock, white wine and vegetables, thickened with egg yolk, finished with Madeira wine, crayfish butter and anchovy essence

Saint-Malo, sauce Sauce *vin blanc* with mustard, shallots and anchovy essence

salmis, sauce A mix of vegetables, game trimmings, white wine and demi-glace sauce, finished with mushroom essence and truffle essence. Served with game

Sauces

smitane, sauce Onions cooked with white wine, sour cream, lemon juice. [also called *smitaine sauce*]

Solferino, sauce The juice from ripe tomatoes mixed with meat glaze, lemon juice and cayenne pepper, finished with maître d'hôtel butter, shallots and tarragon

Soubise, sauce *Béchamel sauce* with a lot of onion purée added, flavoured with nutmeg. Used for roast meats

souchet, sauce The poaching liquor from fish, reduced, mixed with sauce aux vin blanc, garnished with carrot, leek and celery

suédoise, sauce Mayonnaise mixed with apple purée and grated horseradish

suprême, sauce Chicken stock, mushroom trimmings, finished with lemon juice.

tartare, sauce 1) Chopped capers, gherkins and parsley mixed with mayonnaise. Served with fried fish. 2) Mashed hard boiled egg yolks, mixed with vinegar, oil whisked in as if making mayonnaise and finished with spring onions mixed with a little mayonnaise

tomate, sauce *see* **tomato sauce**

tortue, sauce Veal stock with mixed herbs, mushroom trimmings and peppercorns mixed with demi-glace and tomato sauce and finished with Madeira wine, truffle essence and a cayenne pepper

tyrolienne à l'ancienne, sauce Finely chopped onion cooked with tomato and *sauce poivrade*

tyrolienne, sauce Shallots cooked and added to tomato, cooled and mixed with mayonnaise, parsley, chervil and tarragon. Served with fried fish and cold meats

valois, sauce *see* **sauce foyot**

vénitienne, sauce Tarragon vinegar, shallots and chervil mixed with *sauce vin blanc* and finished with green butter, tarragon and vinegar

Véron, sauce *Sauce normande* mixed with *sauce tyrolienne* and finished with meat glaze and anchovy essence

verte, sauce Mayonnaise mixed with tarragon or chervil, chives and watercress.

villageoise, sauce Veal stock, mushroom essence, velouté sauce and *soubise sauce* thickened with egg yolk and cream. Used for white meat

Villeroi, sauce *Sauce allemande* mixed with ham and truffle essence, reduced until very thick

vin blanc, sauce Fish velouté mixed with white wine, butter and cream. Used for fish. [also called *white wine sauce*]

Sauces

vin rouge, sauce   Mix of vegetables, red wine and *espagnole sauce* added; finished with butter, anchovy essence and cayenne pepper. Served with fish

Vincent, sauce   Equal parts of green sauce and tartare sauce well mixed

xérès, sauce   *see*   **sherry sauce**

Sauces

Restaurant Notes

Restaurant:

Address:
Country:
Phone:
Date: Price:
Meal:
Who was present:
Rating: food..../10   wine..../10   service..../10
Notes:

Restaurant:

Address:
Country:
Phone:
Date: Price:
Meal:
Who was present:
Rating: food..../10   wine..../10   service..../10
Notes:

Restaurant:

Address:
Country:
Phone:
Date: Price:
Meal:
Who was present:
Rating: food..../10   wine..../10   service..../10
Notes:

Restaurant:

Address:
Country:
Phone:
Date: Price:
Meal:
Who was present:
Rating: food..../10   wine..../10   service..../10
Notes:

Restaurant:

Address:
Country:
Phone:
Date: Price:
Meal:
Who was present:
Rating: food..../10   wine..../10   service..../10
Notes:

Restaurant:

Address:
Country:
Phone:
Date: Price:
Meal:
Who was present:
Rating: food..../10   wine..../10   service..../10
Notes:

Restaurant:

Address:
Country:
Phone:
Date: Price:
Meal:
Who was present:
Rating: food..../10   wine..../10   service..../10
Notes:

Restaurant:

Address:
Country:
Phone:
Date: Price:
Meal:
Who was present:
Rating: food..../10   wine..../10   service..../10
Notes:

New Terms

Menu Term:
Translation:
Notes:

Menu Term:
Translation:
Notes:

Menu Term:
Translation:
Notes:

Menu Term:
Translation:
Notes:

Menu Term:
Translation:
Notes:

Menu Term:
Translation:
Notes:

Menu Term:
Translation:
Notes:

Menu Term:
Translation:
Notes:

Menu Term:
Translation:
Notes:

Menu Term:
Translation:
Notes: